THE LIBRARY
MARY'S COLLEGE OF MARYLAND
MARY'S CITY, MARYLAND 20686

The
GAY CHURCH

The
GAY CHURCH

by Ronald M. Enroth
Gerald E. Jamison

William B. Eerdmans Publishing Company
Grand Rapids, Michigan

Copyright ©1974 by William B. Eerdmans Publishing Company
All rights reserved
Printed in the United States of America

Library of Congress Cataloging in Publication Data

Enroth, Ronald M
The gay church.

Bibliography: p. 141
1. Church work with homosexuals. 2. Universal
Fellowship of Metropolitan Community Churches.
I. Jamison, Gerald E., joint author. II. Title.
BV4470.E57   261.8′34′157   73-16483
ISBN 0-8028-1543-X

Excerpts from *The Lord Is My Shepherd and He Knows I'm Gay,* ©1972
by Troy D. Perry, are reprinted by permission of the publisher, Nash
Publishing Corporation.

A quotation from *The Other Minorities,* ed. by Edward Sagarin, ©1971 by
Ginn & Co., is reprinted by permission of Xerox College Publishing. All
rights reserved.

Selections from *The Gay Mystique,* Copyright ©1972 by Peter Fisher, are
reprinted with the permission of Stein and Day/Publishers.

Selections from *The Gay World,* by Martin Hoffman, ©1968 by Basic
Books, Inc., Publishers, New York, are reprinted by permission of the
publishers.

Grateful acknowledgment is also made to the publishers for permission to
quote selected passages of the following books:

Deviant Behavior, by Ronald L. Akers; Wadsworth Publishing Company,
Inc., Belmont, California, 1973.

Homosexual Behavior Among Males, by Wainwright Churchill; Hawthorn
Books, Inc., New York, 1967.

Odd Man In, by Edward Sagarin; Franklin Watts, Inc., New York, 1969.

Out of the Closets: The Sociology of the Homosexual Liberation, by Laud
Humphreys; Prentice-Hall, Inc., Englewood Cliffs, New Jersey, 1972.

Contents

Foreword

This book is not a comprehensive survey of gay churches in the United States. It is merely an introduction to the Metropolitan Community Churches (which constitute the first known "gay" denomination) and other, smaller religious organizations that minister primarily to the homosexual community. Nor should it be considered a scholarly treatise, though we draw heavily on the work of scholars from many disciplines and gratefully acknowledge their contribution. We are students of sociology, not theology, and if the book is not theologically sophisticated enough for some readers, we ask their indulgence.

We are deeply grateful to many friends, who directly or otherwise helped make this book a reality. Special thanks go to Lou Ann Sheldon, Dana Alexander, Rod Snider, Michael Leming, Evan Adams, and Robin Wainwright. Our appreciation is also extended to Robert Gundry, Ray Anderson, and George Blankenbaker for their theological and biblical insights. The Enroth household and Westby House exhibited patience and understanding during this entire undertaking and Shirley Gay and Betty Bouslough provided invaluable assistance in preparing the manuscript.

Finally, we would like to thank those individuals who consented to be interviewed by us — or by one of our friends — during the various stages of research that culminated in this book. The cooperation of the Rev. Jim Sandmire is especially appreciated. We only regret that the Rev. Troy Perry, founder of MCC, did not respond to our repeated requests for an interview.

The opinions and conclusions expressed in this book are our own and do not necessarily reflect the views of those who have so graciously assisted us.

Santa Barbara, California   Ronald M. Enroth
                                             Gerald E. Jamison

1: It's a Gay World After All

Not long ago it was taken for granted that "good," "respectable" people did not mention the word "homosexuality" and certainly did not talk about, except in hushed tones, people who were "that way." Society — particularly the church — ostracized these "sex deviates" and considered them moral lepers. Victims of this "affliction" drifted toward the margins of society to form their own little world with a distinctive life-style, jargon, and network of relationships.

Like other minority groups, homosexuals have developed a subculture — a way of life — and a means of coping with the larger society that they see as oppressive. In any major metropolitan center this sub-society, more popularly known as the "gay world," can be found. In recent years this gay world has begun to emerge from the shadows with the help of popular novels, movies, plays, and a score of scholarly books.

Whatever else the liberating sixties and seventies have accomplished, they have increased our fund of information about previously taboo areas of human sexuality, including homosexuality. We hope that this book will provide additional information about a dimension of the

gay world that remains for many an unknown factor —
the gay church. It is not so much a book on religion as
it is a book on homosexuality, and the reasons for that
will become clear as the chapters unfold.

Some will be amazed, if not shocked, to discover that
such a thing as a church for homosexuals even exists,
more so to find out that one gay "denomination," the
Universal Fellowship of Metropolitan Community
Churches, now has over forty congregations in the
United States and is expanding abroad as well. The
Metropolitan Community Church of Los Angeles (MCC-
LA) has had as many as one thousand in attendance on
a Sunday morning. It has formed its own seminary and
has been instrumental in the formation of a gay synagogue that shares its facilities. Its pastor, the Rev. Troy
Perry, has been the subject of features in *Newsweek,* the
New York Times, and other periodicals circulated among
the non-gay or "straight" population. Yet most Americans have never heard of MCC, Dignity, or any of the
smaller religious groups ministering largely to the
homosexual community.

Perhaps the most concise introduction to the gay
church is the text of an invitational leaflet distributed by
the MCC of San Francisco on the streets and in gay bars.

> Today there is a church where the gays and straights worship
> God side by side. Some churches give lip service approval to
> the gay Christian. Yet their members snub the gays. Some
> churches ban the gay person completely. Today there is a
> church which accepts homosexuals as normal persons. That
> church is Metropolitan Community Church. This is a church
> where gay lovers can come to the altar rail together. This is a
> church that has a social life that is geared to the gays. M.C.C.
> is a church where you can renew your childhood faith in
> Christ and yet not hide nor be ashamed of your sexual inclina-
> tions. Why don't you renew your faith in Christ this Sunday
> at M.C.C.?

In the chapters that follow we shall basically elaborate
on that statement. We shall discuss the emergence of the
gay church, its theology, its relationship both to the
straight society and to the homosexual world, the prob-

lems unique to it, and the implications of the gay Christian movement for the Christian church as a whole.

As non-gay observers, we are well aware of the limitations that the outsider role placed on us in our research and writing. Some will claim that it is impossible for heterosexuals truly to understand and interpret the gay world. There is certainly some validity to that charge: no one can fully comprehend or identify with a particular group unless he is a participating member of it. Nevertheless, we have attempted to read widely material written by both gays and straights and have made every effort to research thoroughly the published materials of the various gay religious groups. We have talked with gay pastors, church members, and other leaders of the homophile movement.

The idea for this book came in a sociology class in which one author was student and the other professor. A number of the students decided to do a term project on the Metropolitan Community Church of Los Angeles. Eventually this expanded to include the San Francisco church and research on a much broader scale. For one and a half years we have explored the gay church, including three months of intensive study in San Francisco, which permitted regular attendance at the Metropolitan Community Church there. While we have attempted to remain as objective as possible during this research effort, no such venture can be value-free. As Wainwright Churchill and others have observed, in dealing with a subject as sensitive as homosexuality, one will be lumped with the "good guys" or the "bad guys" depending on the value positions that surface in one's writing.

> Hence the exclusively heterosexual investigator will not always find the same meaning in the very same collection of data that the homosexually or bisexually inclined investigator may find. Indeed, so strong is the persuasion of sexual emotion, and the preferences and avoidances that always cling to it, that it is doubtful if there will ever be a fully objective account of any aspect of sexual life (*Homosexual Behavior Among Males*, p. 9).

Our objective is to present a survey of the gay church and its facets, rationales, and characteristics. The reader will have to make his own evaluation of whether the movement is legitimate, orthodox, and useful.

Before examining the gay church itself, we shall present a brief overview of homosexuality, mentioning the usual explanations of its causes, its incidence in the population, and some of the terms and phrases commonly used in the gay subculture. This background information will assist the reader in thinking through some of the issues to be raised later in the book.

Stated simply, a homosexual is an individual who is sexually attracted to members of the same sex. The chief inadequacy of this brief definition is that it fails both to distinguish between the psychic orientation and the overt behavior and to account for the period of time during an individual's life when he or she can be defined as homosexual or for the strength or degree of that sexual preference.

Behavioral scientists have described human sexuality as a continuum ranging from exclusive heterosexuality to exclusive homosexuality. Some individuals, for example, known as bisexuals, are equally attracted to both sexes. Kinsey and his associates devised a seven-point scale to categorize the relative heterosexual-homosexual preferences of individuals (Kinsey *et al.*, 1948). It is possible, then, as Akers points out in his book *Deviant Behavior,* "to distinguish among degrees of activity, intensity of emotional attachment, or commitment to a homosexual way of life" (p. 154).

The Kinsey study found that 37 percent of the males and 13 percent of the females have at least one overt homosexual experience to the point of orgasm between adolescence and old age. About 4 percent of American males are exclusively homosexual throughout their active sexual life, both in overt experience and psychic response. Added to that is a significant percentage of men who are not exclusively homosexual for their whole lives: ten percent of all American males have had fairly extensive homosexual experience. Homosexuality, thus, affects directly a considerable number of people. Translating the statistics into everyday terms, it is probable that about a third of one's friends, acquaintances, business associates, and fellow church members have been involved in homosexual activity at some point in their lives.

There are many different kinds of homosexuals and they can be found in virtually every social, economic, and religious category. Although stereotypes abound, there is no such thing as a "typical" homosexual. As Martin Hoffman notes, gays

> . . . run the entire gamut from the swishy faggot who can be identified a block away, to the husband, son, or brother whom even the fairly sophisticated person would not suspect of any homosexual interest. They include people who are handsome, clever, and rich, those who are ugly, stupid, and poor, and all combinations and gradations in between (*The Gay World,* p. 33).

Unfortunately, many people generalize about all gay people on the basis of stereotypes of the limp-wristed "fairy" or the hypermasculine female homosexual. Straight society often deduces an individual's sexual preference from personality characteristics and physical mannerisms that may be quite irrelevant. Writing about the often distorted images of male homosexuals, Churchill states:

> It is commonly believed . . . that such males tend to be physically weak and that their body structure resembles that of the female, especially around the hips and thighs. They are supposed to have delicate skins, fine complexions, and high-pitched voices, along with obvious hand movements, peculiarities of gait, and other effeminate mannerisms. Artistic interests are ascribed to all these males and they are also said to be temperamental, emotionally unbalanced, over-sensitive, difficult to get along with, and undependable (p. 40).

Some homosexuals do conform to the stereotypes, but they are clearly in the minority. Effeminacy is not a highly valued trait in the gay world; masculinity is. In his book *The Gay Mystique,* Peter Fisher explains that until recently, many young homosexuals entered gay life well aware of the widespread myth of their supposed effeminacy. "They tried to match themselves to the myth, affecting characteristics they supposed to be typical of homosexuals. Trying to live up to the expectations of the role provided for them, they bécame much as society expected them to be" (p. 70).

Fisher sums up the whole question succinctly:

> Stereotypical thinking is difficult to avoid. As soon as one makes a generalization, he risks losing sight of diversity. No generalizations can validly be made about homosexuals as a group, except that they prefer members of their own sex as sexual partners. At the same time, various distinct types of gay people can be found in the gay world. The discussion of different types of people need not, however, imply stereo-types, if we keep in mind that the search for similarities often produces an artificial blindness to differences (p. 73).

Another mistaken notion is that homosexuals don't really know which sex they are, and that male homo-sexuals secretly wish to be women. To quote Fisher again:

> The vast majority of male homosexuals see themselves as men and the vast majority of female homosexuals see themselves as women. Few would have things any other way. . . .
> Male homosexuals are attracted to other men, not because they see themselves as or wish to be women, but simply be-cause they find other men sexually exciting. The feeling of sexual attraction is the same, whether one is heterosexual or homosexual (pp. 74-75).

Much less has been written about lesbians (female homosexuals) than about male homosexuals. Their image in the mind of the public is less clearly defined, although the stereotype of a "mannish" woman generally prevails. People are less suspicious about two women living together than about two men sharing an apartment. Similarly, women seem to be allowed more freedom in expressing affection toward one another. They are per-mitted to embrace in public, whereas such behavior between males is unthinkable, except perhaps after an important athletic victory.

Lesbians also identify with a community or subculture of their own. Their subculture, however, appears to be much less important for them. Hoffman points out that there are relatively few lesbian bars and that female homosexuals do not use bars in the same way that males do. "They rarely pick up partners for one-night stands but, rather, engage in a kind of courtship ritual which is very much like that of heterosexual couples" (p. 165). Thus lesbians are thought to be much less promiscuous than male homosexuals.

Generally speaking, there are fewer mannerisms and behavioral cues associated with female homosexuals than with their male counterparts. A few lesbians adopt male mannerisms and prefer masculine dress. This type of lesbian is often referred to as a "butch" or "dyke" and is stereotyped as being the "active" sex partner. The more feminine-appearing and supposedly more "passive" lesbian is called a "fem."

There appears to be some overlap between the male and female homosexual subcultures. To some extent this is found in the gay liberation movement, and especially in the gay church. In recent years many lesbians have also identified with activist groups in the women's lib movement. Gagnon and Simon found that almost all the lesbians they interviewed "included some male homo-sexuals among their friends" and that "for some of the lesbians male homosexuals constituted their only close male friends" (*Sexual Deviance,* p. 273). Many homo-sexuals, of course, have non-gay friends who do not know of their sexual orientation.

Transvestites are persons who wear the clothes of the opposite sex. Transvestism is not an exclusively homo-sexual phenomenon; indeed, some figures would indicate that 96% of transvestism occurs among heterosexuals. Nor is it limited to men. Fisher notes: "Many straight people assume that all homosexuals are transvestites, that all transvestites are homosexuals, and further confuse the issue by believing that both homosexuals and transvestites wish to be women. The real situation is quite different" (pp. 75-76). Transvestites should not be confused with transsexuals, who want to become, physiologically and psychologically, members of the opposite sex. Such transformation is usually achieved by means of sex-reassignment surgery. Most transsexuals deny being homosexual.

No discussion of the topic of homosexuality would be complete without raising the difficult question of causation. How can we explain homosexual behavior and what is its origin? What processes are involved in the development of a homosexual orientation? Is a person born gay? These are complex yet extremely significant issues. Psychiatrists, sociologists, and psychologists have written many pages of often confusing and sometimes conflicting information about homosexuality and its genesis. Clearly no single, all-encompassing "cause" can be found in the medical and professional literature, and much more research is needed to clear up some continuing puzzling questions. In the scope of this discussion we can only summarize briefly some of the major explanatory approaches taken and elaborate on one which seems to be gaining in acceptance and which, to us, makes the most sociological sense.

First, there are those who stress physiological and biochemical explanations; a person is born with certain hormonal or other biological characteristics that would make him become homosexual. Studies purporting to show evidence of this frequently have been based on small samples from the population, and the various findings are often contradictory. Akers states flatly:

> Investigations designed to uncover congenital, neurological, biochemical, or chromosomal differences or anomalies in homosexuality have failed. . . . Examinations of physical type, blood and urine samples, color blindness, taste threshold, and skin grafts have revealed no differences between the habitually homosexual person and the heterosexual person. . . . Attempts to detect some anomaly of the chromosomal structure in homosexuals have failed . . . (p. 155).

Although there is no consensus on the question within the homophile community, many gay people, including those in the gay church, strongly affirm that homosexuality has an hereditary or constitutional basis. However, from the researchers in the field

> we hear less and less about heredity and constitution as more and more data which show that sexual preferences of any kind are acquired rather than inherited become available. Nevertheless these theories are still favored by some clinicians, as well as by a great many preponderantly homosexual males who feel that they were "born that way" (Churchill, p. 93).

The type of explanation that receives perhaps the most attention in both the popular and professional literature is psychiatric and psychoanalytic theories. In brief, these theories suggest that homosexuals suffer from some underlying pathological condition, usually traceable to early childhood experiences and to parent-child relations in particular. Critics of this idea maintain that while parent-child interaction may well explain neurotic behavior in *some* homosexuals, it cannot be applied generally as a cause of homosexual behavior in all gay people. Churchill notes that "complicated psycho-dynamic accounts of the origin of this behavior may find some limited applicability in certain isolated instances, but such accounts can hardly explain homosexuality in the majority of instances in which it occurs" (p. 95).

It is common in medical circles to label homosexuality as a "disease," a form of mental illness. One of the first psychiatrists to attack this concept of homosexuality was Dr. Martin Hoffman. In his book *The Gay World* he asserts that homosexuality *in itself* does not necessarily indicate mental illness. He claims that many of the books on homosexuality by psychiatrists are based on studies of a sample that is not necessarily representative of the homosexual community. "Homosexuals seen in psychiatric treatment are no more representative of homosexuals in the general population than are Jews seen in psychiatric treatment representative of all Jews" (p. 157).

The hostility of gay people for the psychiatric profes-

18 THE GAY CHURCH

sion is well known. At the annual convention of the American Psychiatric Association in 1973, the issue of homosexuality as a diagnostic category was debated. According to a report in the gay newspaper *Advocate,* one gay activist pleaded with members of the APA's Nomenclature Committee to "take the damning label of sickness away from us. Vote a resolution of this convention to take us out of your nomenclature of psychiatric disorders" (June 6, 1973, p. 12).

At the same convention, Dr. Judd Marmor, a professor of psychiatry at the University of Southern California and vice president of the APA, presented what the *Advocate* termed "a clearly pro-gay speech."

> "Surely the time has come for psychiatry to give up the archaic practice of classifying the millions of men and women who accept or prefer homosexual object-choices as being by virtue of that fact alone mentally ill.
>
> "Let us base our diagnoses of psychiatric disorders on clear-cut evidence of serious ego-dystonic feelings or irrational behavior and not on the fact that life-styles happen to be out of favor with existing cultural conventions" (p. 12).

The approach to understanding and explaining homosexuality we shall follow is based on the concept of social learning. We agree that sexual object-choice is basically a learned phenomenon; in Hoffman's words:

> It is . . . related to many factors which act upon the individual's development during all phases of his life. With such a complexity of interacting relationships, it would, of course, be impossible to identify a single cause for homosexual preference (p. 128).

Nevertheless, we can examine the process by which sex-role behavior is acquired. Every known society expects men and women to behave with systematic differences, and American society is no exception. Powerful social forces shape sex roles, and this process of what sociologists call "sex-role socialization" is continuous and extends into adulthood.

> Being masculine in American society includes being attracted and attractive to women; it is an approved and expected com-

> ponent of the male role. Likewise, the conventional expectation of those playing the female role is that they will be sexually attuned to men. This strong cultural definition of the place of sexuality in the male and female roles leads to the popular stereotype of the homosexual as somehow "feminine" and the lesbian as "masculine," and it is also related to the special contempt for the homosexual who completely reverses roles (Akers, pp. 147-148).

Learning the behavior appropriate to one's sex role begins early in America. Parents' choice of toys helps insure that boys will be boys and girls will be girls, though there is usually greater pressure on boys than on girls to evidence the behavior appropriate to their sex. Fathers in particular are anxious that their young sons not become "sissies." On the other hand, as Udry points out, "American culture is not nearly so restrictive in eliminating masculine items from the behavioral repertoire of the young girl" (*The Social Context of Marriage,* p. 67).

Why is it, then, that the majority of people grow up to become heterosexuals and only the minority engage in homosexual behavior? Is it correct to say that some individuals are born with at least a tendency or predisposition toward homosexuality? Wainwright Churchill provides this answer:

> It is more correct to say that humans . . . have a capacity for heterosexual response and a capacity for homosexual response at birth, but that they do not have an inborn tendency toward either heterosexuality or homosexuality. After the drive has been conditioned one way or the other or both ways — in other words, after the *capacity* for response has been exploited and learning has begun — we may speak of a *tendency* toward heterosexuality and/or a tendency toward homosexuality. But this tendency is *acquired* and is a product of learning rather than a part of the individual's biological inheritance (p. 105).

Such learning is often unconscious. Sex roles, attitudes, and emotional responses are usually learned quite apart from any formal tutelage. Again, the insights of Churchill are helpful:

To an appreciable extent almost all of us have been conditioned to respond to or avoid various sexual stimuli long before we have ever experienced direct erotic contact with another human being. Indeed, it is this earlier, vicarious form of conditioning which usually determines the nature of the first overt contacts. The effect of earlier conditioning tends to push us toward the sort of erotic contact with which we have already learned to associate gratification (p. 108).

The sexual socialization of most people effectively shields them from homosexual opportunities. They grow up being rewarded for conforming sexually, and they would expect to be punished for showing homosexual inclinations (Akers, p. 149). Some — whether consciously or inadvertently — are exposed to unconventional sexual experiences. The introduction to homosexuality may occur in a sex-segregated institution like a prep school. Or it may happen quite by chance. The person may or may not derive sexual satisfaction from the first encounter. But if these initial experiences are sexually pleasurable, they are likely to be repeated and perhaps reinforced through masturbation. This may lead the individual to seek out other sexual partners with like interests. Someday he may "come out" — identify himself publicly as a homosexual and enter the gay world.

2: Father Troy
and Mother Church

The lead article in *The Catalyst,* newsletter of the Metropolitan Community Church of Denver, asks: "Who is Troy Perry??" The writer answers that "he is the one man who has done more than anyone else anywhere at any time to help gays both individually and as a community" (March 26-April 9, 1972). Considering the fact that Troy D. Perry was virtually unknown in American religion and in the gay community prior to 1968, that is a notable statement.

Perry is the founder and, until recently, the pastor of the Metropolitan Community Church of Los Angeles, known affectionately in MCC circles as the "Mother Church." He also serves as General Moderator of the Universal Fellowship of Metropolitan Community Churches and has become something of a patron saint in the gay liberation movement. Sociologist Laud Humphreys, in his book *Out of the Closets,* describes Perry as a "powerful and articulate" speaker:

His round face dominated by a broad grin, the husky Pentecostal preacher evidences more charismatic features than any other leader produced during the homophile movement's first 20 years. . . . In theology he is "fundamentalist," in

attire a Catholic, but by conviction, Troy Perry is also a political activist, manifesting both the street skills and the special
innovative and verbal skills of the gay subculture. He has
proved himself a master of confrontation strategies (p. 150).

Without Troy Perry there would be no MCC. Perry
firmly believes that God singled him out at an appropriate time in history to start a new denomination as an
outreach to the gay community. In his homespun and
sometimes melodramatic autobiography, *The Lord Is My
Shepherd and He Knows I'm Gay* (Nash Publishing,
1972), Perry states that MCC was founded "so gays
would have a place to worship God in dignity, and not
as lepers or outcasts, but as His creation, as His
children" (p. 222).

The autobiography begins on a mystical note somewhat
prior to Perry's birth:

> One thing is certain about me! I feel that I have a total sense
> memory that predates my birth by a good long time. It's like
> being a seedling soul in two parts, your mother's and your
> father's genes. I have an awareness of having been a seedling
> — a physical presence in my father's sperm and in my mother's
> ovum before they united (p. 10).

His admitted fascination with mysticism and sense of
fate reappear in his account of a chance meeting with a
black woman minister who happened to believe in "spirit
guides." The woman claimed that she could actually see
a person's guide, and on meeting Perry she told him that
his "guide" had manifested himself as an Indian wearing
a clerical collar. Did Perry have a deceased relative who
was a minister? Did he have any Indian ancestors? He
responded that he was part Cherokee Indian on his
father's side of the family and that he did in fact have a
deceased great-uncle who had been a Pentecostal minister. The woman, a complete stranger to Perry, went on
to predict, "God has a ministry for you" (Perry, p. 113).

Troy Perry was born into a large Southern family of
pioneer stock in Tallahassee, Florida, in 1940. His earliest
years were very happy ones dominated by a father he
deeply loved and respected. The family's religion he

characterizes as rigidly Pentecostal, an influence that was to leave an unmistakable imprint on his own future ministry. One of his favorite preachers during those early years was his Aunt Bea, a one-time prostitute turned Pentecostal preacher. Sister Bea became pastor of the Nashville River Holiness Church, a congregation that practiced snake-handling and speaking in tongues.

> She never wore makeup, she never cut her hair, and she wore long sleeved dresses. She was sedate. She was odd, but she was widely respected. . . . She must have had a tremendous influence on my early religious searchings. It is an influence that stays with me now (Perry, p. 43).

At the conclusion of one particularly emotional service, in one of her less sedate moments, Aunt Bea laid hands on his head and exclaimed that she had a revelation from God:

> She smiled and told them that God has His hands on me, and that He was going to use me mightily in His ministry. She swore to them, and to me, that I had been called by God to preach. She placed her hands back on the top of my head. "God has His hands on this boy," she told us all. . . . A hush hung so heavy over the congregation you could feel it. Tears welled into my eyes. Why did I cry? I don't really know. I was afraid, but I felt a happy weight of oncoming responsibility (Perry, p. 47).

Perry's father, a prosperous bootlegger, was killed in an auto accident when Troy was still a young teen-ager. The death was to have a profound impact on the family, especially on Troy, the oldest of five children. In the years that followed, Mrs. Perry worked hard to keep her family intact through a series of unsuccessful marriages and financial troubles. The closeness that grew up between Perry and his mother at that time persists to this day:

> There are people who would tell you that a homosexual is overly attached to his mother — too fondly so. I don't feel that I am. I have her with me, now, as much as I can, because I want to repay a debt that I've owed her for such a long time.

I owe her my life, and so do my brothers owe her theirs. We're just saying thank you in our own way (Perry, p. 56).

In her foreword to the autobiography Mrs. Perry admits that she once had a "traditional reaction" toward homosexuality, but now, she says, "I'm with him all the way."

> In our background, everything was a sin. And it surely took a lot of thinking and praying to really realize that many of the old strict ways in which we were raised just aren't what it's all about. The real sins are hate and being inhuman to each other. That's how we all sin against the homosexuals. I'm glad that I've been able to discard that attitude in my life. I've met the nicest people that I've ever met in my life as a result of Troy's work (pp. viii-ix).

"Mom Perry," as she is called by the Los Angeles congregation, was the subject of a special Mother's Day tribute in the May 1973 issue of *New Life,* the official publication of MCC-LA. She still enjoys preparing an old-fashioned Southern home-cooked meal, the article states, and she manages to devote four or five days a week at the church offices answering telephones and doing whatever needs to be done.

Troy Perry believes that homosexuality is preordained by God. "I'm sure that homosexuality was in my genes, and in my soul, from the very beginning" (Perry, p. 10). He admits that he can offer no scientific or theological support for this contention — "I just believe it, that's all."

> Sometimes I think it's just like catching the brass ring on the merry-go-round. I guess if you follow the law of averages, those who catch the brass ring turn out to be homosexuals. Well, I caught the brass ring (p. 10).

While Perry sees the origin of his homosexuality in the context of some kind of divinely sanctioned genetic probability game, his autobiography makes a fairly good case for the view (briefly mentioned in Chapter 1) that homosexuality involves a process of social learning in which the role of life situations and even chance elements in one's experience may be significant. In his book Perry details his first homosexual encounters as a teen-

ager with friends of the family or chance acquaintances.
A seventeen-year-old friend named Daniel is especially
singled out as one who first introduced him to sexual
activity.

> Daniel had coal black hair that laid in thick locks over his
> forehead, like a cascade. . . . His smile was so winning.
> Daniel was a Biblical beauty. His lips were kind of a dark red.
> I remember them as a blur of scarlet. He walked so surely
> and proudly. . . . Later on as we grew older we had other
> times together. We began to branch out a little. There were
> other kids my own age, and we all experimented as much as
> we could (Perry, pp. 23, 25).

Perry's stepfather's younger brother moved into the
household, and once brought a young sailor friend home
for a brief visit. The sailor proceeded to make sexual
advances toward Perry. When he was sixteen, he had
occasion to continue his experimentation at a youth camp
run by a Pentecostal church. He found himself bothered
by self-doubt and guilt feelings about his sexual urges.

> I think I wanted to know how others felt. I wanted to know
> . . . what the other boys were doing about it. That curiosity
> drove me to more experimentation with homosexuality. I kept
> asking, "Why me, God? Now, why, God, did you call me, and
> yet I have these feelings? Why do I have these attractions to a
> fellow?" I had the conflict between my feelings and what the
> church taught (Perry, p. 58).

Perry was granted his first license to preach at age
fifteen by a Baptist church in Winter Haven, Florida.
He was convinced that God had called him to preach
and that he had to find a girl friend. He left the Baptist
church and found a girl — the pastor's daughter, in fact
— at a Pentecostal church. As time went on, Perry was
increasingly distressed by intense emotional feelings,
fantasies, and drives that he could not fully understand.
More and more he found himself turning away from a
heterosexual orientation, becoming what he terms a
"semiheterosexual." Yet he wanted to become a minister
and so he decided that marriage would be a means of
resolving his dilemma.

After three months of dating another girl, who played the piano at a church he attended, Perry proposed. Nine months later they were married. They were both eighteen at the time. Soon after the wedding they left for Chicago, where Troy enrolled in a Bible college. It wasn't long after they had settled in their new home that an old friend of his — a gay friend — stopped by for a visit and attempted to have sex with Perry. The word got out when Perry's friend talked to the officials of the small church Perry was pastoring in Joliet, Illinois. Confronted with the information, he was asked to leave town.

> I felt so dirty. That's why I hate the word queer so much. I felt the crushing stigma of being known as a queer. It hurt then. Now it wouldn't. I have a perfect defense against that kind of cruelty, but then, it was on a plane so revolting that no one could talk about it, nor even pray about it. Not once did they say, "Can we pray for you?" — nothing except, "How quick can you get out of town?" I was so bowled over (Perry, p. 68).

After a difficult attempt at explaining the situation to his wife Gloria, Perry decided that they should return to Florida. He became the pastor of a little rural church in Lake Alford, and their life seemed to return to normal. Their first son was born. But once again the past surfaced to plague him, and he was forced to resign from the church. He and Gloria returned to Illinois, where Troy enrolled in night courses at the Moody Bible Institute, took a job with a plastics firm, and pastored a congregation associated with the Church of God of Prophecy, a denomination similar to the Church of God, with which he had previously been associated.

Then the company for which Perry worked offered him a junior executive position at a new plant in Torrance, California. He moved his family to Southern California, where he was soon invited to pastor a Church of God of Prophecy congregation in Santa Ana. "We all trod the straight and narrow. No deviation from doctrine. No movies. No dancing. No smoking. No drinking. No nothing" (Perry, p. 76).

After the birth of their second son, Gloria took the

two children on a trip East. While she was away, Troy happened across some books and magazines on homosexuality. One book, *The Homosexual in America,* by Donald W. Cory, had a particular impact on him:

> When I finished the book, I knew without the shadow of a doubt that I was a homosexual; I was gay. And there was just nothing for me to be afraid of any longer. This was it. I could honestly look at myself in the mirror, and say to myself, "You know something, you're a homosexual." And it didn't upset me (Perry, p. 78).

Convinced that he could no longer deny his homosexuality, he made an appointment with the district overseer of his church. He explained his problem to the man, who passed it off as a "trick of the devil" and suggested they pray about it. Perry responded, "This'll sound kind of funny, but it doesn't work. I've prayed until I'm blue in the face about this, and God just doesn't seem to understand, or He doesn't answer my prayers about this for some reason" (p. 80). After they had prayed anyway, the overseer admonished him to go back to Santa Ana, "tear up that book, and forget about all of this nonsense" (p. 80). He went back, but he did not tear up the book or forget what it had said to him.

> I picked a nice looking man out of my congregation; I was sure he was gay. It turned out he also hustled. I just walked up to him and said, "How would you like to stay over and spend the night with me tonight? My wife's back East, and she's been gone quite awhile." He gave me a long, knowing look and a big smile and said, "Why sure, if you promise not to molest me" (Perry, pp. 80-81).

When his wife returned home, Perry admitted to her his homosexual orientation. Gloria suggested that the two stay together and try to work things out, but Troy knew that was impossible. Soon Perry's bishop learned of the situation. He immediately arranged a congregational meeting for that night, and called to tell the young pastor:

> We've called all the church members and they'll be at the meeting tonight. All we want from you is to just get up and say that you feel like you failed the Lord and that you're resigning

and then you can leave. And they'll never know why you're leaving. And we'll appoint the new minister to take your place right after that (p. 82).

He followed the script as directed, went home and told Gloria that they no longer had a congregation, and that it was all over. In one of the more moving sections of his book, Perry discusses what happened immediately following their decision to separate:

We knew that we were tearing up five years of our lives together. And we were dissolving our family. My oldest boy, "little Punkin" we called him, kept asking why we were doing this, why we were moving, and most agonizing, why we were crying. . . . I packed them up in the car, and took them to the terminal so they could take a bus back to the Midwest and be with her parents. . . . There was to be no more future for us together. . . . I kissed both of my boys goodbye. . . . I went back to my car and got in and just went all to pieces. . . . I had closed a chapter in my life that is, even now, painful to recall (pp. 83-84).

There followed a period of several years of further exploration of the gay scene with its night spots, special jargon, and network of friends and lovers. Despite his professed homosexuality, Perry was inducted into the army. After serving a two-year hitch, he received an honorable discharge and returned to Los Angeles, where he took a job with a well-known department store. He made the rounds of Hollywood gay meeting places and experienced his "first really open love affair with another man" (Perry, p. 98).

. . . I had fallen out of love with God. Benny was my new object of worship and adoration. I idolized him. The sun rose and set in him, in Benny. That was just it. No one could love me the way he did. And I couldn't love anybody else the way I loved him (Perry, p. 100).

But the affair was brief and ended in near tragedy. Spurned by his lover, Perry attempted suicide by slashing his wrists with a razor blade. He was rushed to a hospital where, on recovering, he remembered God and asked his help. As he tells it,

> I studied the Bible, especially the Old Testament. I began to
> reevaluate everything I had ever learned. There were so many
> contradictions and so many ideas. I found that you can prove
> or disprove anything by citing the Bible, and especially, the
> Old Testament, or St. Paul in the New Testament. But the Lord
> was guiding and directing me.
>   I'm sure that He had put me through all of this in order to
> better equip me for my mission. He was beginning to set in
> motion the vision I needed for what I had to do, what I had to
> accomplish in this life (Perry, p. 109).

A series of events, coupled with a growing sense that
it was God's will for him to start a church for homosexuals, led Troy Perry to advertise the first service of
the Metropolitan Community Church of Los Angeles,
held in the living room of Perry's house, in the *Advocate,*
the newspaper with the largest circulation in the homophile community. The meeting was scheduled for October 6, 1968, and Perry had no idea how many would
show up. Twelve people finally arrived for that first
Sunday service. After telling the assembled group a little
about himself and his pastoral background, Perry unveiled
his hopes for the new church:

> I said the church was organized to serve the religious and spir-
> itual and social needs of the homosexual community of greater
> Los Angeles, but I expected it to grow to reach homosexuals
> wherever they might be. I made it clear that we were not a gay
> church; we were a Christian church, and I said that in my first
> sermon (Perry, p. 122).

From the very beginning, the church grew phenom-
enally. Soon, Perry's house could not contain the parishioners, and the congregation began a series of moves —
first to the Embassy Auditorium, then to the Encore
Theater, where Willie Smith, the church's songleader,
worked as a projectionist. For over a year and a half
the congregation had use of the theater virtually rent-free.
Finally, in late 1970 an old church building was located
at Union and 22nd Streets, in a poorer section of Los
Angeles populated mainly by Blacks and Mexican-
Americans. The building was purchased and plans were
made for the extensive remodeling that was necessary.

One Sunday while they were still worshiping in the Encore Theater, Perry challenged his flock to bring in $10,000 for the building fund by the following Sunday. During that week Perry prayed and fasted. So convinced was he that God would honor his faith that he brought a twenty-gallon trash can to collect the donations.

> We would all march by and give what we could. We would march row by row and give. I asked if someone could play that old-time hymn, "Give Me That Old Time Religion." Someone rushed to the organ and . . . Willie Smith stepped up and, in his own Aimee Semple McPherson style, took the microphone and led the congregation in verse after verse. It ignited the whole group. Hands clapped. Feet stomped. The faithful marched. They came by emptying pockets, paper bags and coffee cans, and tossing checks, bills and coins into that trash can (Perry, p. 194).

After marching up and down the aisles, the congregation calmed down long enough for a communion service while the treasurer counted the offering. As soon as it was announced that it had exceeded ten thousand dollars, the entire congregation again exploded with emotion and applause. Shouts of "Thank you, Jesus!" filled the theater. The secular gay press reported the moment as "a vindication, as if the homophile community had just signed its declaration of independence, or won its spurs, or captured the Bastille" (*Advocate,* December 1969). Troy Perry's confidence was at an all-time high. "Now I knew we could not be stopped," he exulted (p. 195).

The Mother Church was officially dedicated on Sunday, March 7, 1971. Over a thousand people received engraved invitations to the gala event. By now MCC was big news in the gay community, and articles in national magazines and newspapers had let the straight world as well know about Troy Perry and his accomplishments. The church was packed for the dedicatory service. Telegrams of greetings were read from notables who were unable to attend, including one from Governor Ronald Reagan. Commented Perry: "He can't come to visit us, but I'll be visiting him on June, the twenty-fifth in Sacramento.

On that date I will hold a peaceable demonstration marching from San Francisco to the capitol in Sacramento, to protest against the antiquated sex laws" (Perry, p. 204). Also present was sociologist Dr. Evelyn Hooker, who had chaired the National Task Force on Homosexuality for the National Institute of Mental Health.

During the service of dedication, Willie Smith sang "The Impossible Dream," from *Man of La Mancha*. Doubtless the lyrics were appropriate to the occasion. Pat Rocco, a leading producer of homosexually oriented films and a one-time staff photographer for MCC's denominational magazine *In Unity*, sang "The Lord's Prayer." The congregation sang a rousing rendition of the gospel song "He Lives" as well as "Eternal Father, Strong to Save."

This somewhat unconventional admixture of various types of church music is characteristic of MCC-LA. Troy Perry is the first to admit that there is something for everyone at the Mother Church. Each service is something of a performance, with Perry's old-time fundamentalistic background coming through quite clearly. Before the 11 a.m. worship service gets underway on a typical Sunday, the congregation is led in a kind of gospel singing warm-up time by Willie Smith. Smith steps front and center, the spotlights focused on his invariably white outfit — Sunday morning a white gown, Sunday evening white trousers and a bright shirt — and vigorously directs the assembling congregation in such favorites as: "When the Saints Go Marching In," "What a Friend We Have in Jesus," "Do Lord," and "How Great Thou Art." When this latter gospel hymn is sung, the group will often join hands, raise them over their heads and sway from side to side, in Jesus-people fashion.

At eleven o'clock the formal procession enters the sanctuary, including Troy Perry in his black robe and white cassock, and other members of the ministerial staff along with guest participants. The worship service itself combines elements of a liturgical format with informality that includes jokes and laughter, applause, Amens, and folksy, "down home" expressions like, "Isn't Jesus wonderful?" This diversity dates from the early days of the church, when the format of the worship services was being developed. The need for flexibility resulted from the tremendous variation in church background of the parishioners.

> We utilized the books of worship from the Episcopal, Presbyterian and Lutheran churches as well as those that members of the congregation wanted considered. We experimented and we accommodated. It may sound like a hodgepodge, but what emerged was a straight line of well organized ritual that allows for improvisation or change should any occasion within the church warrant it (Perry, p. 130).

To the outsider and first-time attender, a service at MCC-LA seems to be as much entertainment as worship of God. Gay jokes and other references to the gay world are not uncommon and lend the impression that this is indeed a "gay church," despite protestations to the contrary. Pastor Perry's sermons are simple, brief, often meandering, and sometimes punctuated by humorous anecdotes and illustrations. They support his own observation that he is not an intellectual. "I have never claimed to be the type of speaker that required the listeners to bring a dictionary to each session" (Perry, p. 126). Charles Lucas, who assisted Perry in writing his autobiography, sums up Perry's charisma in a Postscript:

> His hold over an audience is hypnotic. Here was a born leader with a dedication to his mission. Here before his congregation stood a showman out of the same mold as the pulpit greats of the past such as Aimee Semple McPherson and Billy Sunday. Energy flowed from Troy Perry and ignited his entire congregation (p. 230).

Perry's Southern background is no doubt an asset to him in the same way that the homey, folksy illustrations and Southern accents of Billy Graham and Oral Roberts appeal to people and help them communicate with the average man-on-the-street. In an exaggerated sense, Perry's sermon delivery resembles that of these two famous evangelists, though they are poles apart in certain crucial areas of doctrine and biblical interpretation. On the other hand, Perry does boast that the gifts of tongues and miraculous healings are sometimes present in his church, and a Pentecostal atmosphere pervades many of the meetings. During one service Perry remarked: "You'll have to excuse me if my Pentecostal background is showing, but today I feel like I want to pull up my skirts and shout 'Praise the Lord!'"

Also evident to the outside observer is Perry's tendency to communicate his pleasure with the publicity that both he and the MCC congregations are receiving and the growth the denomination is experiencing. He travels a great deal, visiting the new and established churches in the Fellowship. Yet in the pulpit, at home or away, he manages to convey the idea that his journeys are not all that burdensome. One Sunday he told the assembled faithful that he had granted an interview with a *New York Times* reporter and that a special article would be appearing in the following Sunday's edition. Another featured article, he added, would be published in London.

A typical Sunday morning service will include a time when prayer requests are received from the congregation, some of which will be for lovers who are ill or traveling or having family problems. Music will be provided by the Chancel Choir or the Metro-Chords. Following the sermon, communion is administered. For this more solemn part of the worship service, the congregation files to the front of the sanctuary to partake of the elements. It has become traditional for gay couples — both lesbians and male homosexuals — to walk hand in hand down the aisle and kneel together to receive the sacrament. As they return to their seats, members of the congregation will sometimes wave at an acquaintance or stop briefly to kiss a friend seated on the aisle. Non-gay visitors have sometimes reported that during the administration of communion the participating ministers appear to be unusually physical, sometimes fondling the ears or the neck area.

After communion Perry closes the service in prayer

and invites all to adjourn to the Social Hall for coffee and doughnuts. Leaving the church, the visitor will encounter a table where several publications, records, and trinkets are for sale, along with copies of the *Advocate*. This self-styled "Newspaper of America's Homophile Community" contains not only news articles and editorials pertaining to the gay community, but also ads for gay bars, baths, massage parlors, and sex literature. The MCC justifies this, like the bar ministry, on the ground that it is necessary for maintaining contact with and awareness of the gay community they are attempting to reach for Christ.

Flipping through the *MCC News,* an official publication of the Los Angeles church, one notices reminders and invitations to coming social events, such as the wedding at the church of two women or the All-Church Dance, sponsored by the Metropolitan Players. "Our theme will be *In the Good Old Summertime,* so be there in your casual attire — shorts, tank tops, swim suits, or whatever — and be ready for the Fun and Surprises!" Another issue of the *News* announces that MCC is on the air. Perry writes, "This is only a start, with God's love and help, we will syndicate nationally, and we are now preparing our television shows for national syndication" (March 5, 1972). The same issue contains news of MCC's Samaritan Bible Seminary and a brief profile of a 25-year-old seminarian. "Statistically, he is 6'0" and weighs in at about 185 pounds. Blue eyes and blond hair are features that catch particular attention of this handsome and extremely personable young man." Also noted is the upcoming appearance at the church of the Caltech Glee Club, consisting of 55 male voices.

Parish news in a typical issue included an account of the South Central Parish Dinner/Show.

> The dinner consisted of roast leg of lamb, steamed carrots, fruit cup, baked potato with butter and fruit punch. The show was the Dating Game. Contestants were drawn from ticket stubs and 3 games were played. . . . The prizes for the dates

were 2 trips to Palm Springs and 1 was to a private cottage in the mountains (Nov. 28, 1971).

Also included were these "Words of Wisdom":

> Do not smoke in the Church. I finally learned this for *God* gave me a gentle but painful reminder the other day. I came trampsin in, lit cigarette and all (flying in as I usually do — Not Fairy Style — Please!!!) and tripped on the carpet and cut my lip. So don't smoke in the church for God may also remind you.

If MCC's church services are folksy and humorous, so are the church publications. The August 1971 issue of *MCC News* contains a cartoon with the caption: "If a guy's got good legs, he SHOULD wear hot pants." In any given issue of a newsletter, one is likely to find peculiar juxtapositions — a short "Know Your Bible" type article, complete with expressions like "ISN'T JESUS WONDERFUL?", standing opposite an ad for a bar that provides "adult refreshment for those who love their fellow men."

Describing the church a reporter for the *MCC News* wrote: "No meeting is so somber, no service so weighty, no topic so awesome, that it cannot be punctuated by laughter" (Nov. 28, 1971). That attitude comes out most clearly in the evening service. On a typical Sunday night, Willie Smith leads singing that is even more boisterous than in the morning, most of the songs being choruses from a mimeographed sheet: "Everybody Ought to Know," "For God So Loved the World," "Thank You Lord For Saving My Soul," and other fundamentalist favorites. Smith sometimes parades up and down the aisles with his little white microphone in hand while the congregation claps to the music. Troy Perry, casually dressed, asks for testimonies. He may then comment on the diversity of denominational backgrounds at MCC, asking members of specified denominations to identify themselves by raising their hands. Present are large numbers of Roman Catholics and Baptists and a scattering of Methodists, Presbyterians, Episcopalians, Pentecostals, Mormons, and even Jews. Visitors in the audience are introduced and acknowledged by applause. Finally, seated on the steps near the altar, Rev. Perry gives a brief and informal talk. Included may be bits of gay humor and allusions to the jargon of the subculture ("Jesus freaks and Jesus fruits").

At the conclusion of one service we attended, Perry gave an altar call and a number of people went forward, some emotionally, others to pray quietly. Rev. Perry closed the service with the announcement that details of MCC participation in the Christopher Street West parade (a gay lib event) would be given at the hamburger fry in the Social Hall following the service. (He later asked for twenty volunteers to wear "MCC T-shirts" in the parade.)

Displayed on tables in the Social Hall were various advertisements about gay beauty contests and plays. On one table there were photographs of Troy Perry's recent wedding to Steve Jordan, a Roller Derby skater. Orders were being taken for these photos. In his autobiography, Perry describes his first meeting with Steve Jordan:

> If ever there was a type that really turned me on here it was standing right in front of me. He was a young, wiry, small American of Mexican descent. His hair was a luxurious shining coal black, almost blue, color. He had rather limpid dark brown eyes. His lips were full and sensuous. He had a rather impish grinning smile that won me completely. His skin was a flawless candy caramel color. I just went all watery inside (p. 142).

As the fourth anniversary of MCC-LA approached in October 1972, things were going quite well for Troy Perry and his church. Attendance had mushroomed from the original twelve to 800 or more at a Sunday morning service, making it the third largest church in Los Angeles. The church and its pastor had become a political force in the Los Angeles area and were in the forefront of the struggle for gay liberation. It had established a 24-hour Crisis Intervention Center, a ministry to the deaf, and a thriving youth group called the Kool-Aids.

Suddenly tragedy struck. On January 27, 1973, an early morning fire heavily damaged the sanctuary and the church offices of the Mother Church. The building was virtually destroyed and the remaining portion condemned by the city. The blaze was initially reported as being "of suspicious origin," but according to an account published in the February 24 edition of the *Los Angeles Times,* investigators later determined that the fire was not incendiary. Arson was, however, the cause of a $100,000 fire that destroyed San Francisco's Metropolitan Community Church in late July 1973. Apparently prayer books were used as fuel.

Insurance covered part of the loss of the Los Angeles church building, but a building fund was established with a view toward relocating and building on a new site. MCC took out a full page ad in the *Advocate,* featuring a photograph of a stern-faced Troy Perry standing with arms folded amid the wreckage of the burned out sanctuary. The appeal for funds read in part:

> . . . we believe we CAN change the world! We will NOT be stopped! To those people who would rejoice because of our loss: WE SERVE YOU NOTICE — that we, in the Gay Community, will never permit the hands of the clock to be turned back on us ever again! We WILL rebuild and go forward. . . . FROM THE FLAMES . . . WE RISE TO BUILD AGAIN (February 28, 1973).

Six weeks later Perry reported in the *Advocate* that $13,000 had already been raised, some of it from bar owners and those "who say that they are not church people, but who believe in what we are doing" (April 11, 1973).

The loss of the Mother Church represented a crisis for the entire gay denomination, as was evidenced in an appeal to the membership of the Metropolitan Community Church of New York City in their magazine, *The Gay Christian.*

> How will we respond to this tragedy? We can wring our hands and pull out our hair crying "Oh, woe is us! It just doesn't pay to come out of our closets!" . . . and develop a self-depreciating attitude of defeat. We can assume that "It's a Los Angeles problem; let them worry about it!" . . . Or we can recognize it as

a challenge to the entire gay community and a tremendous opportunity to exhibit our mettle. People will be watching how
WE respond to this crisis, because it IS a crucial pivot point
in the gay Christian movement (February 1973).

The new temporary location of MCC-LA became the
Aquarius Theater on Sunset Boulevard in Hollywood,
remembered for the long-running production of *Hair*
and earlier for broadcasts of the popular radio show,
"Queen for a Day." The vacant theater was made available to MCC for only a minimal maintenance charge.
Evening services were being held at the HELP (Homophile Effort for Legal Protection) Center. At the time of
this writing, the Sunday morning service has returned —
after a brief stay at the American Legion Hall — to the
Encore Theater in Hollywood. Attendance seems to be
down.

On May 6, 1973, Perry announced that he was stepping
down as pastor of the Los Angeles church in order to
devote full time to the concerns of the denomination as
a whole. In an article in the *Advocate* his new role was
described as being in part that of a "troubleshooter" for
the fellowship, and an expansion of his existing respon-
sibilities as Moderator of the denomination.

"I'm not going to desert the flagship. . . . It's going to have my
attention the same as any church would under similar circum-
stances within our Fellowship. But, of course, I would lie to
you if I said that I didn't have a special feeling for the Mother
Church, because I do. I spent five years here, and some of the
best memories of my life have been situated around this church
and its group of people" (June 6, 1973).

When Perry's resignation became effective on October
7, 1973, he also received the title of "Pastor Emeritus"
by special action of the Board of Directors. Now that the
charismatic young pastor has officially departed, many
will speculate on the future of MCC-LA.

3: Gay Church in a Straight Jacket?

Despite the sociological and cultural support the gay church has enjoyed, success in Christian circles is likely to be measured first of all from a theological framework. Aware of this, homosexual Christians have undertaken the task of constructing what might be called a gay theology. What has emerged, slowly, has often been disjointed and unsophisticated, for the Metropolitan Community Church can boast of few capable theologians in its ranks and as a result has been forced to turn to eager but unschooled church members. (The term "gay theologian," which appears throughout this discussion, refers loosely to a religious apologist who is homosexual himself.) Roy Birchard, editor of MCC-New York's magazine, *The Gay Christian,* explains the situation with pride and confidence.

> For while we are not tenured academics, the writers here share the attitude that being who we are has contributed to our views of conventional religion, and has sometimes made insights available to us that we might not otherwise have known. All of us have read theology and worked at it from time to time. So now we are attempting to do some ourselves to advance the self-understanding of our community (*The Gay Christian,* September 1972).

Thus gay Christians begin the defense of their faith.

A critical problem surfaces immediately. Religious

homosexuals are no more of one single theological per-
suasion than their heterosexual counterparts. And when
liberals and fundamentalists, radicals and evangelicals
try to amalgamate in one fellowship, open disagreements
over biblical interpretation soon follow. The result is
many theologies with little hope that a uniform statement
can be found to offer a straight church eager to judge.

Many gay Christians have no trouble dismissing the
Scriptures as dated, irrelevant, and incompatible with the
twentieth century, choosing rather to create their own
standards. Such liberals experience a comparatively small
degree of contention from like-minded straight denominations and similarly gain the tacit approval of the secular gay community. This does not rest comfortably with
evangelical gay Christians who, perhaps surprisingly to
some readers, constitute the majority in the movement
today. Led by the unswerving fundamentalist Troy Perry,
MCC has cast its lot with this camp and has chosen to
do battle with Bible in hand. When this unwritten rule
is violated, it is quickly corrected, as in a Denver case
involving a columnist who called the inspiration of the
Scriptures into question. Charles David had no more than
alluded to the fallibility of human authors, especially
Paul, who was "divinely inspired on a lower level," when
Pastor Bob Darst interrupted in print:

> The editor of *The Catalyst* would like to take exception to Mr.
> David's opinion that not all of the Scriptures are divinely in-
> spired. Every portion of the Old and the New Testament —
> every single verse of every chapter of every book is most defi-
> nitely the divinely inspired Word of God (*The Catalyst,* March
> 11-25, 1973).

Classic fundamentalism therefore is unquestionably the
foundation for gay theology. Many of the religious liberals
in MCC congregations merely bypass the struggle of
Scriptural rationalization that their conservative brothers
must face. Rev. John Hose (MCC-San Diego), for example, is content to argue from a neo-orthodox, progressive revelationist position out of the mainstream of
theological debate:

> I am not a person who is given to try to rationally expound my
> views by quoting Scripture back to people who quote me Scrip-
> ture, because I think you can quote Scriptures *ad infinitum*.
> You pick a topic and I can take something out of context and
> prove it by the Bible — the rightness or wrongness of it. I
> believe in continuous revelation. I think God reveals his will to
> mankind just as possibly today as He did in the first century
> A.D. I don't think St. Paul was the only one who could have
> a revelation.

Gay theology, it is easy to see, is formless at best.
MCC's by-laws make no mention of homosexuality, nor
has the church released any official statement on gay doctrine. Thus, our analysis of it must be fairly elementary.
Homosexual Christianity has satisfied itself with proof-
texting and rationalization rather than wrestling with
Scripture. So, its theology as presented here can only be
as complete as its church has developed it to this point.

Gay theologians make the initial claim that sexuality
is neither right nor wrong, it is simply a gift from God.
To be heterosexual or homosexual is not a question of sin
or morality, but rather the product of God's infinite mind.
For reasons unknown he has assigned all of mankind to
one of the two sexual roles. Our only responsibility is to
accept his decision. This argument, of course, relies solely
on the validity of the constitutional or genetic theory for
the cause of homosexuality. The gay person therefore
must be enlightened to the point of accepting his sexual
orientation. He must "come out," no longer hiding his
homosexuality with shame but rather pronouncing it
boldly and with pride. In the New York church a "liturgy
of coming-out" is under development, which, like baptism,
will mark this important spiritual phase in the life of a gay.

The emotions of self-acceptance are related by Valerie
J. Valrejean, editor of MCC-Seattle's newsletter, *The
Paraclete:*

> Something new happened to me the other day; something I
> had never dreamed could ever possibly happen: I wept tears of
> joy and rejoiced in God that He had made me gay. . . . So really
> I feel that my gayness is a gift from God that I can use to fur-
> ther His work. I only hope and pray that we Christian homo-

sexuals will not be found guilty of hiding our gift away (in
our closets?) like the slothful servant in the parable of the
talents, but that we will use it to further the work of God and
add unto His glory (*The Paraclete*, December 10, 1970).

The fact that the homosexual condition is, in fact, a
gift from God is reportedly borne out in verses such as
the following:

And God saw everything that He had made, and behold, it was
very good (Gen. 1:31).

It is He who has made us, and not we ourselves (Ps. 100:3).

Homosexuality as genetically and divinely caused is apparent from the Scriptures, gay theologians say. If this
is true, then (they argue) it would be against God's will
to attempt a change from one's present sexual role. As
the prophet Jeremiah asked: "Can an Ethiopian change
his skin, or a leopard its spots?" (13:23). For the gay
Christian, a three-verse progression in the Bible (1) af-
firms God's calling of man to different sexual states, (2)
discourages any rejection of that calling, and (3) requires thanksgiving for God's gift. The formula is as
follows:

For there are eunuchs who have been so from birth, and there
are eunuchs who have been made eunuchs by men, and there
are eunuchs who have made themselves eunuchs for the sake
of the kingdom of heaven. He who is able to receive this, let
him receive it (Matt. 19:12).

Brethren, let each man remain with God in that condition in
which he was called (I Cor. 7:24).

For everything created by God is good, and nothing is to be
rejected if it is received with thanksgiving (I Tim. 4:4).

The customary interpretation, supported by the context,
would relate the verses only to the married/celibate state,
but the homosexual interpretation is convincing to a gay
person searching for self-justification.

It is Jesus Christ who calls to himself the gays whom he
created. Jesus always addresses himself to those who are
lost, never recognizing the sexual state of any individual.
The woman in adultery and the prostitute were the objects of his uncondemning love. Troy Perry repeatedly

preaches to his congregation the message that Jesus is calling them, a point established firmly in his autobiography.

> Not once did Jesus say, "Come unto me, all ye heterosexuals — who have sex in the missionary position with a member of the *opposite* sex — and you can become true followers." No! Jesus said, "Come unto me, all ye that labour and are heavy laden, and I will give you rest." And that includes homosexuals, too. God does not condemn me for a sex drive that He has created in me. He doesn't condemn me unless I leave the areas of love and go into the areas of destructive, excessive, lust (Perry, p. 153).

Furthermore, Perry maintains, it was Jesus who died for his sins, and thus it is only Jesus who had the authority to make the unconditional invitation of John 3:16. "I'm not saved by the blood of Paul!" The letters of the apostle and missionary are usually dismissed in gay theology, for it is Paul who is the most condemning of homosexual activity among New Testament writers. Jesus never condemned anyone; instead he shared the fact that all of our actions should be guided by one thing only — love. The call is a return to the teachings of Jesus, the one individual who was infallible.

> Pick up an edition of the Bible with Christ's recorded statements printed in red. Study only His words, comparing His positive approach with the often negative approach found elsewhere throughout the Scriptures. Notice His emphasis on love — His silence on the means of sex, but concern only with the motives behind it.

> Can we actually believe a Christ of such love, a Christ who recognizes the human need for mortal love and its physical fulfillment as well as for His divine love, can ask that legions of homosexuals either live a life of celibacy or else face eternal damnation? Not the Christ I know (*Homosexuality: What the Bible Does . . . and Does Not Say*, Kim Stablinski).

Gay spokesmen are quick to cite Paul's remark that some of what he wrote was merely his own opinion and not to be taken as a commandment from the Lord.

Indeed, Jesus Christ revolutionized the world with love. Unrestricted sexual behavior — as long as it can be subjected to the ultimate test of love — is therefore allowable. Christ came to teach us to love, and MCC has learned his lesson well. Pastor John Hose, for example, considers the physical act of sexual intercourse in itself an expression of love.

> I'm not saying that every time someone cohabits with someone that these have to be people who are in love, but I think it is an act of love. If I love you, one of the ways in which I can demonstrate it is by loving your body as well as your spirit or soul. The fact that some people prefer to do it with their own sex, rather than the opposite sex, happens to be our bag. We're entitled to it.

Gay Christians point out that lust is completely unacceptable in their theological framework. Whenever one individual exploits another, that is undeniably sin. In this light the gay activity that MCC encourages can only be viewed, according to gay theology, as God-ordained and blessed. To this can only be added the two verses that have come to find cornerstone prominence in homosexual Christianity:

> I know and am persuaded in the Lord Jesus that nothing is unclean in itself (Rom. 14:14).

> To the pure all things are pure (Titus 1:15).

As if the theology needed further support in the minds of most homosexuals, the gay church has attempted to bolster its position by pointing to the hypocrisy of the straight church. If it can be proved (they reason) that heterosexual Christians fail to keep their own standards, there will be little room for them to point a condemning finger. Thus gay Christians ask the straight church why women are allowed to speak in church (contrary to I Cor. 14:34-35); why long-haired men are not dismissed (despite I Cor. 11:14); why women are not forbidden to wear jewelry (as is stated in I Tim. 2:9-10); and why divorcees may remarry (against the requirement of I Cor. 7:10-11). If these texts are not maintained literally, how can the specific passages regarding homosexuality demand adherence? Such discrimination, gay theology argues, is nothing less than oppression.

As a result, gays can boldly present what has been termed by New York churchman Steve Wolfe an "unnatural theology" (taken from Rom. 1:26). As homosexual Christians, they can truly say that they have surpassed what is "natural" in both the sexual and spiritual spheres. And this is the fulfilment of God's desire — that his people be set apart, that is, unnatural. Wolfe worded it succinctly, "As a non-reproductive form of sex, homosexuality testifies to our God-given vocation to transcend the laws of nature" (*The Gay Christian,* September 1972).

Recently, religious thinkers in the homophile community have begun to identify with contemporary theologies of liberation. When James Cone, in his *Black Theology of Liberation,* maintained that God is black to the black man, a convenient model for the gay world was born. Just as Jesus spoke liberation to the social lepers of his day, so he speaks to homosexuals in the twentieth century. Freedom — a key word in the New Testament — is prominent in the vernacular of gay theology. The Rev. Howard Wells of New York, a former Navy lieutenant who had no church background before becoming an MCC pastor, writes:

> If we call on God to deliver us from our bondage, if we willingly and unequivocally place our lives in his hands, we can expect to be liberated and to be free to develop our full potential as human beings. It says that God has chosen to make the gay condition, his condition; he is not neutral in this struggle but rather, is on our side. . . . To say that God is gay means that he understands us and approves of the way he made us (*The Gay Christian,* September 1972).

Wells goes on to say that the God conceived of by the straight church "is not the God I know, but is rather an oppressive idol. I reject it. . . ."

For most Christians, the question is to be decided in the context of the specific references to homosexuality in the Bible. Twelve passages in the Old and New Testaments refer, implicitly or explicitly, to homosexuality. The first of these is often considered most influential in justifying society's abhorrence of homosexual practices. Genesis 19:1-28 tells the story of God's anger toward Sodom and Gomorrah because of their grievous sins. Abraham, seeking to save the cities, was allowed to search for ten righteous men. If he was successful it would divert God's intentions to destroy them. Thus God sent two emissaries — angels dressed as men — to Sodom, where they would lodge with Lot, Abraham's nephew. Hearing of their arrival, the "men of Sodom, both young and old, all the people to the last man" surrounded Lot's house demanding that he produce his guests "that we may know them." Lot refused, even offering his two daughters to appease the mob, but the crowds were insistent, at which point the angels blinded them. In the morning both cities were destroyed.

The interpretation focuses on the meaning of the Hebrew verb *yadha* (to know). Gay theologians contend that this word is used only ten times in the Old Testament to denote sexual activity (without exception referring to heterosexual coitus), whereas it appears more than nine hundred times to indicate a gesture of hospitality. Furthermore, there is a specific Hebrew verb — *shakhabh* — used directly to describe homosexual activity; thus, there is no linguistic argument that *yadha* necessarily carries a sexual connotation. They assert that the word could best be translated "get acquainted with" in the account of Sodom's destruction. In the four other Old Testament accounts of the destruction of Sodom there is no mention of homosexual activity: Isaiah 1:10; 3:8-9; Ezekiel 16:49; and Jeremiah 23:14 list the reasons for God's anger as the cities' failure to listen to the Lord's teaching, their insolent parading of their sin, their failure to aid the poor and needy, their pride, idleness, laziness, falsehood, and adultery. Homosexuality is noticeably absent from the catalogue.

A passage in Judges 19-21 closely parallels the Sodom incident. In this later account an unnamed Levite enters the town of Gibeah seeking without success a place to spend the night. Finally, an elderly field laborer invites the Levite's party to his home. When the townspeople hear of this they surround the house, beating on the door and crying, "Bring out your guest that we may know him." The host offers them his daughter and his concubine. They say no, but when he shoves the latter out of the door, the men, as a last resort, "had relations with her and abused her all night."

Some gay theologians use this to support the view that the primary sin in both instances was the violation of the Oriental custom of hospitality. When the townspeople of Gibeah and Sodom realized their failure to be hospitable, it is argued, they reacted bitterly against both the ones who had offered and the ones who had received the proper hospitality. They chose rape as the means of punishment and humiliation in both cases — homosexual rape that was thwarted entirely in the Genesis account and satisfied heterosexually in the Judges story. Compared to the true sin of inhospitality, the sexual attack was of only minor significance. Other interpreters bypass such complexities and argue that the sin was unquestionably lust, which is wrong whether it is found in a gay or straight framework.

Evangelical theology challenges the gay interpretation on several points. The linguistic argument that *shakhabh* would have been used if a sexual connotation had been intended passes without serious consideration, for both verbs can be used to convey similar sexual meanings. It is the context that must provide the key to interpretation; and to purport that in this passage *yadha* can best be translated "get acquainted with" is a travesty of hermeneutics. The "hospitality" argument falters on grounds of logic. If the Sodom crowd were merely intent on meeting the strangers, it would have been illogical that Lot would offer them his daughters, with whom they were undoubtedly already familiar. Such a move could not have been expected to satisfy the crowd. Similarly, the description of an enraged mob scarcely comports with our ordinary picture of a "greeting party," and Lot's obvious reference to the virginity of his daughters indi-

cates the sexual emphasis in the situation. The Judges'
account does in fact point to the importance of the
Hebrew law of hospitality, but it cannot cover the obvious reference to homosexuality. A plausible explanation
for attempted homosexual rape hardly justifies such
activity.

Perhaps the most accurate interpretation of the event
is that Sodom was destroyed on account of the intensity
of its sin, part of which was rampant homosexuality.
When speaking to their generations, the prophets Isaiah,
Ezekiel, and Jeremiah referred to those sins of Sodom
which were particularly applicable to their specific situation. In similar manner Jude, in his epistle (vs. 7), mentions Sodom as populated by those who "indulged in
gross immorality and went after strange flesh." Thus if
the sin of the era was pride, it would naturally be mentioned; if it were immorality, then the sexual sins of
Sodom would be highlighted. The Jude verse is conveniently overlooked by gay theologians, as is the fact that
the first Jewish interpretive writers and the early church
fathers unequivocally labeled the sin of Sodom as "sodomy" — homosexuality.

In the case of five references to "Sodomites" (in the
King James Version of I Kings 14:22-24; 15:12; 22:46;
II Kings 23:7; and Deuteronomy 23:17-18) there are
references to what apparently was a flourishing fertility
cult in Jerusalem. More recent translations of the Bible
have cleared up a misunderstanding in this area. Whereas it appeared on a reading of the King James Version
that God was condemning homosexuals (sodomites), the
Revised Standard Version correctly translates the object
of divine judgment as "male cult prostitutes." Straight
and gay theologians alike are content to forgo discussion
on these five passages; the former see the issue of little
importance and the latter point to it as another case of
distinguishing between love and lust.

The two other Old Testament references to homosexuality are included in the Levitical Holiness Code.
They are:

You shall not lie with a male as with a woman; it is an abomination (Lev. 18:22).

If a man lies with a male as with a woman, both of them have committed an abomination; they shall be put to death, their blood is upon them (Lev. 20:13).

There are three basic ways gay theology tries to invalidate the apparent divine condemnation here: by appealing to human reproduction, cult purification, and the hypocrisy of the straight church.

In the first chapter of Genesis God commanded, "Be fruitful and multiply" (Gen. 1:28); later he promised Abraham that he would make his descendants as numerous as the sands of the sea. Procreation was thus received as a divinely appointed task by the children of Israel; consequently, any form of population limitation was strictly forbidden. This was emphasized by the judgmental slaying of Onan (Gen. 38:9) for his practice of birth control. So, too, homosexuality, as a form of birth control, is condemned. Paul Roberts excuses this aspect of the law of Moses on "human reproduction" grounds, drawing support for his theory from the rather broader range of behavior deemed morally acceptable in biblical times. To foster population increase, the Lord encouraged practices that would now be judged immoral. David, the great king of Israel from whose line Jesus was born, enjoyed at least five wives at the same time. Solomon had seven hundred wives and three hundred mistresses. But the command to multiply has long since been fulfilled, Roberts argues. Homosexuality is perhaps being a God-given answer to the problem of population explosion:

God commanded Noah to build an ark, but when the ark was finished we would not expect Noah to keep on building. God told Moses to make a large powerful nation, and laws condemning birth control were necessary until the goal was accomplished.

Today the population explosion may bring destruction. Man is limited to one wife at a time and the Bible even suggests that men ought not to get married if they can keep from it.

The Bible now says, "It is good for a man not to touch a woman" (*Sodomy and St. Paul*).

The appeal to cult purification to invalidate the Levitical condemnations notes that the forbidding of homosexuality is imbedded in a long list of prohibitions, many of which seem unreasonable to us. For this reason it is assumed that the Levitical Code was constructed merely to intensify Israel's sense of national "holiness." That is to say, there is nothing sinful in itself about what is prohibited; rather, these divine directives are merely intended to separate God's people from the surrounding nations. One activity was not necessarily more moral than the other, but can only be described as different.

The third appeal — to the straight church's hypocrisy — evolves from the second. Although it is the least sophisticated of the three approaches, it is the standard answer to be found in the MCC biblical apologies. This is undoubtedly due to its origin with Troy Perry. In his autobiography he outlines the classic defense as presented to a Los Angeles pedestrian who had just attacked him with her purse for his offer of a gay tract:

> She looked me over, backed off a step, and I thought she was going to hit me again. She said, "Young man, do you know what the Book of Leviticus says?"
>
> I told her, "I sure do! It says that it's a sin for a woman to wear a red dress, for a man to wear a cotton shirt and woolen pants at the same time, for anyone to eat shrimp, oysters, or lobster — or your steak too rare."
>
> She said, "That's not what I mean!"
>
> I said, "I know that's not what you mean, Honey, but you forgot all of these other dreadful sins, too, that are in the same book of the Bible" (Perry, p. 150).

The argument is simply that straight Christians have no right to pick and choose which prohibitions are to be obeyed.

A few comments might be made in response to this threefold line of reasoning. In the first place, the "human reproduction" theory falls significantly short of explaining the Leviticus references because of the penalty attached. Capital punishment for those unable to reproduce is totally incongruous if God's sole desire was to populate the earth, for no purpose would be served by his destroying those who, for biological reasons, fail his plans. In like manner, the cult purification interpretation is unacceptable to evangelical theologians. It is impossible to reduce the homosexual reference to positive terms. If homosexual activity were indeed acceptable in God's sight, and prohibited for Israel merely to separate them from other nations, there would not be the accompanying label of "abomination." In the same light, it is difficult to interpret the practices forbidden in the prohibitions that immediately surround homosexuality — incest, bestiality, and child sacrifice — in a similarly positive light, though such an interpretation would seem to be indicated if standard rules of biblical interpretation are followed. By reducing homosexuality to a single category — whether birth control or cultic attribute — gay theology limits the discussion and isolates it from the whole of Scripture.

But what of the view that dismisses the Levitical prohibitions on the ground of the hypocrisy of the church for ignoring some and observing others? A preliminary distinction can be made between God's moral and ceremonial laws according to differences in punishments. Eating rabbit, for example, required only the declaration of "unclean"; the act of homosexuality required death. On this line of reasoning one has no right blithely to assume that homosexuality, which once carried the ultimate punishment, is now acceptable.

A more positive approach, one more in keeping with traditional Christian theology, is to admit that Perry's indictment is to the point. His demand that all the law must be obeyed if any section is heeded is correct as far as it goes. But the Christian world believes that it is no longer bound to the Mosaic law (Col. 2:13-16). Having learned from the precepts given at Sinai at one time, God's chosen people now enjoy through Christ a freedom within the New Testament teachings. The old laws are judged by the New Covenant. This necessarily shifts the discussion from the Levitical prohibitions to the New Testament references to see whether they verify or reject the spirit of the Mosaic laws regarding homosexuality.

The biblical passage undoubtedly most often quoted in reference to homosexuality is Romans 1:26-27:

> For this reason God gave them up to dishonorable passions. Their women exchanged natural relations for unnatural, and the men likewise gave up natural relations with women and were consumed with passion for one another, men committing shameless acts with men and receiving in their own persons the due penalty for their error.

Ironically, this classic basis on which fundamentalist Christianity condemns homosexuality is the very passage gay Christians cite to affirm their activity. They contend that the key phrases to be noted are "exchanged natural relations" and "consumed with passion." Arguing from the constitutional theory of the origin of homosexuality, gay Christians emphasize that they have never turned from a "natural" heterosexual condition to an "unnatural" homosexual one. Quite the contrary, if they were to force themselves to become *heterosexual,* it would be in complete violation of their nature. Furthermore, they maintain that their gay relationships cannot be characterized by the phrase "consumed with passion." Rather, they are loving freely and sincerely and, of course, naturally. What in fact is referred to, they argue, is the practice of hedonistic heterosexuals who are not content with the pleasures of their own sexuality and so turn to (what is to them) the unnatural state of homosexuality.

A second explanation of this passage argues that homosexuality itself is not sinful, but rather punishment for sin. Since God "gave them up" to the homosexual condition as punishment for their sinful nature, the argument runs, the only godly response possible is to endure the chastening of the Lord with a joyful spirit.

The response of evangelical Christianity is that neither

of these interpretations is tenable. If it is left to the individual to subjectively determine what is "natural" for himself, it is argued, the biblical standard is invalidated. Biblical scholars agree that the Romans passage explicitly condemns homosexual practices. The German theologian Dr. Klaus Bockmühl describes the "punishment theory," on the other hand, as "more than naive" (*Christianity Today*, February 16, 1973, p. 14). Bockmühl explains Paul's remarks as completely in harmony with the Old Testament idea that God can punish a sin by delivering the sinner over to it completely. Homosexuality, thus, is unequivocally labeled as sin.

The other two references in the New Testament to homosexual behavior are perhaps the clearest and, as a result, the least discussed in gay literature.

> Do not be deceived; neither fornicators, nor idolaters, nor adulterers, nor effeminate, nor homosexuals, nor thieves, nor covetous, nor drunkards, nor revilers, nor swindlers, shall inherit the kingdom of God (I Cor. 6:9-10, NASB).

> Realizing the fact that law is not made for a righteous man, but for those who are lawless and rebellious, for the ungodly and sinners, for the unholy and profane, for those who kill their fathers or mothers, for murderers and immoral men and homosexuals and kidnappers and liars and perjurers, and whatever else is contrary to sound teaching (I Tim. 1:10, NASB).

The gay apology is reduced at this point to semantics. Those persuaded by gay theology maintain that the term in Timothy which is translated "homosexual" has alternately been translated as "them that defile themselves with mankind" (King James Version), "sexual perverts" (Today's English Version), and "pervert" (J. B. Phillips and New English Bible). They reason that such phrases in no way characterize their life-styles. Perversion and sexual orientation are two separate things, and the latter is never to be judged by the former. If such were the case, heterosexuality could be condemned by the very existence of rapists and child molesters.

But the literal Greek meaning of the word translated "homosexual" *(arsenokoitai)* is specifically "a male who

lies with a male." There are no qualifications or modi-
fiers for the act that Paul is describing here. Lust and
perversion are not necessarily involved. The physical
act of sexual intercourse between two males — despite
any degree of love that may be manifested — is listed
as a sin on par with kidnaping and murder and pro-
hibitive of participation in the Kingdom of God. It is
important to note that Paul is clearly referring only to
homosexual activity, not to homosexual orientation or
tendency.

Furthermore, the Corinthians passage not only indis-
putably condemns homosexual practices but also proclaims liberation from them. Following the judgment of
homosexuals cited above, Paul writes:

> And such were some of you; but you were washed, but you
> were sanctified, but you were justified in the name of the Lord
> Jesus Christ, and in the Spirit of our God (I Cor. 6:11).

This strikes a sensitive chord in the lives of most gay
Christians. Adamant in their belief that they were fore-
ordained to be homosexual and that a "cure" is neither
desirable nor right, they find their views opposed to the
teaching of Paul. The question is: if homosexuals in the
early Christian church were washed, justified, and sanc-
tified, can anything less be required of homosexuals
today? Gay theology maintains, however, that sexual
change is impossible. "Converted" homosexuals are
explained as not having been true homosexuals in orientation, or ones who have undergone effective, but
unnecessary, self-discipline. Homosexuality's alleged
incurability is supported by neither Scriptural nor medical knowledge, and thus the issue is commonly ignored.
For Troy Perry, though, the matter is simple. "I'll
agree," he states. "Paul did not like homosexuals."

Perhaps the most fascinating aspect of gay theology
for straight church members is the interpretation of seven
relationships recorded in the Bible as homosexual. These
are the most effective support for the gay life-style in
the minds of many homosexual Christians. In each case,

inference is involved, for there is no biblical statement of a homosexual union.

Ruth and Naomi are thought by some to have been lesbians. The Book of Ruth recounts the love between the two women, including phrases like "she kissed her," "Ruth clung to her," and "she lived with her," which are seen as indicating a physical dimension to the relationship. To be consistent with the gay life-style, however, the story would more accurately be described as a heterosexual who became homosexual who became bisexual.

Perhaps surprisingly (given his remarks cited above) St. Paul is considered to have established a spiritual-sexual union with Timothy. Supporting this is the contention that Timothy represents a typical gay syndrome, with absent father and strong mother (II Tim. 1:5). According to many, Paul's relationship with the young man strongly resembles the Greco-Roman "male tutor" of that period, a role that clearly had homosexual overtones. Furthermore, it coincides with Paul's unmarried state and his negative views toward marriage. On this view, Paul, a middle-aged adult, enjoyed a younger companion — typical of many gay relationships — and affectionately referred to Timothy as "my beloved" (II Tim. 1:2). Other evidences of Paul's alleged homosexuality are his introduction of the kiss of greeting (Rom. 16:16), and his subjection to the hugs and kisses of a loving mob in Ephesus (Acts 20:37). Finally, Paul opened the last letter to his young lover before his death with these tender words, "As I remember your tears, I long night and day to see you, that I may be filled with joy" (II Tim. 1:4).

The Bible's first brothers — Cain and Abel — are seen as providing history's first case of homosexuality — and incestuous homosexuality at that. The pertinent verses are Genesis 4:6-7:

And the Lord said unto Cain, Why art thou wroth? And why is thy countenance fallen? If thou doest well, shalt thou not be accepted? And if thou doest not well, sin lieth at the door. And unto thee shall be his desire, and thou shalt rule over him.

The gay interpretation of this passage is that God gave Abel a sexual desire for Cain, just as he had given Eve a heterosexual desire for Adam:

Unto the woman he said, I will greatly multiply thy sorrow and thy conception; in sorrow shalt thou bring forth children; and thy desire shall be to thy husband, and he shall rule over thee (Gen. 3:16).

Evangelical Christians use that verse to point out that it is proper for a wife to have a sexual desire towards her husband; homosexuals contend that same-sex desires are likewise ordained of God in Genesis 4:7. The striking parallel between the phrases with "desire" and "rule" seems to speak plainly of this fact. Yet the argument for a Cain-Abel homosexual union is limited to the King James Version of the Bible, which mistranslates the passage. The Revised Standard Version renders the original more accurately.

If you do well, will you not be accepted? And if you do not do well, sin is crouching at the door; its desire is for you, but you must master it (Gen. 4:7).

It was *sin* that desired Cain, not his brother Abel.

An equally interesting relationship centers around the New Testament figure who has come to be known as "the gay centurion." In Matthew 8:5-13, one of Jesus' healings is described as performed on a centurion's "servant." Some state that this is a direct reference to the youthful lover of an officer in the Roman army, a common situation in biblical days. The story continues to show how Jesus, astounded by the faith of this Roman homosexual, not only did not condemn the gay condition, but went out of his way to heal his young lover. The validity of such an interpretation is based on the Greek word Matthew uses for "servant" — *pais,* meaning either "youth" or "servant," with the context determining the more accurate connotation. An examination of the same story in the Lucan account, however, leaves no room for doubt that "servant" is the correct reading here. In Luke 7:2-10, the Greek word used is *doulos,* simply meaning "servant." Thus the possible reference "youth," a word that triggers the imaginations of gay Christians, is eliminated.

Inevitably the question arises whether Jesus was a homosexual. To our knowledge no gay theologian has ventured to contend that he unquestionably was, but many have alluded strongly to the possibility. Troy Perry, despite his denial of a gay Jesus, nevertheless presents some tantalizing inferences to eager homosexuals and startled straight Christians.

> According to the way you [straight people] think and act He would have been a real weirdy — for you. If He lived in this day and age, the way you people label individuals, you would have labeled *Him* a homosexual right off the bat! I don't believe that Jesus was a homosexual. But I know you people. Here was a guy that was raised by a mother with no father — typical of the homosexual syndrome, according to so many psychiatrists (for what that's worth) — He never married, and ran around with twelve guys all the time. Not only that. He wasn't above having bodily contact with another man: John the Beloved lay on the breast of Jesus at the Last Supper. Not only that, but a guy betrayed Him with a kiss! Doesn't that make you want to throw up? (Perry, p. 152).

It is John who is commonly mentioned as the possible gay lover of Jesus, with the specific references to Christ's mention of the young disciple as the one "whom Jesus loved." The gay world, of course, considers that such love is always sealed sexually. It is only fitting that the man who never condemned homosexuality (in reality, never referred to it) and who spoke of all things as summed up in love would commit his widowed mother to his faithful lover John.

More recent speculations about the life of Jesus have led to talk of a second possible homosexual relationship for him — with Lazarus. This idea, based heavily on analysis of a noncanonical ancient manuscript, has already been the object of intense scrutiny in the gay world.

John (with, as one gay writer comments, "no hint of jealousy") is the only biblical author to relate the raising of Lazarus from the dead. He notes that the death of the young man caused Jesus to weep to such an extent that those around took his love for Lazarus to be of a very personal nature (John 11:35, 36). A newly published book, *The Secret Gospel: The Discovery and Interpretation of the Secret Gospel According to Mark* by Morton Smith, develops this relationship more fully.

Smith, an Episcopalian priest and Columbia University history professor, maintains that Jesus may have spent a night in spiritual and physical communion with a man whom he had rescued from death. He bases this on a letter attributed to Clement of Alexandria (A.D. 215) which quotes a supposed secret gospel composed by Mark after the death of Peter, which was meant only for those being initiated into the inner mysteries of Christianity. The letter was discovered in the Greek Orthodox monastery at Mar-Saba near Jerusalem in 1958. The passages of interest are quoted in a recent *Advocate* article entitled "Jesus Christ . . . Supergay?"

> And straightaway going in where the youth was, he stretched forth his hand and raised him seizing his hand. But the youth, looking upon him, loved him and began to beseech him that he might be with him.
> And going out of the tomb, they came into the house of the youth, for he was rich. And after six days Jesus told him what to do and in the evening the youth comes to Him wearing a cloth over [his] naked [body]. And he remained with Him that night, for Jesus taught him the mystery of the kingdom of God. And thence, arising, he returned to the other side of Jordan (*Advocate*, July 4, 1973).

Smith believes that this is the original account of the resurrection of Lazarus written by Mark to explain the secrets of Jesus to young converts. The initiation ceremony began with water baptism administered by Jesus to chosen disciples, singly, and at night. The disciple's costume, as indicated by the fragment passage, was a small linen cloth which was removed prior to immersion.

Now in a pure state, the youth would become united with Christ in spirit and ascend with him into the heavens. At that point the spiritual union was completed by physical union. The further suggestion has been made that such an initiation was included in the night vigil in the Garden of Gethsemane. This rite was interrupted, however, by the intrusion of soldiers and the arrest of Jesus. The initiate on this occasion was the unidentified young man who in the New Testament account of the betrayal "escaped naked" (Mark 14:51, 52).

If those six alleged homosexual relationships in Scripture are considered "possible" by gay Christians, the case of Jonathan and David is seen as a settled issue. Gay theologians exalt this couple as the prime biblical example of two homosexuals in union. The following aspects in Scripture are taken as support for this view.

(1) David never had a successful relationship with a woman.

(2) He loved Jonathan as his own soul (I Sam. 18:1).

(3) Jonathan made an intimate covenant with David (I Sam. 18:3).

(4) Jonathan stripped himself before David (I Sam. 18:4). (It is interesting to note here that at least one MCC congregation considers such a verse to be a basis for ministers to practice nudity.)

(5) Jonathan "delighted" in David (I Sam. 19:1).

(6) Saul accused his son of being perverted because of this closeness to David (I Sam. 20:30).

(7) David and Jonathan kissed one another and wept (I Sam. 20:41). At this point it says that David "exceeded" (KJV). Robert Sirico, pastor of the MCC-Seattle, comments that the Hebrew word here means "to make great," which is perhaps a derivative of the word for "orgasm." In reality, the reference is that David "exceeded" Jonathan in the amount of tears shed.

(8) "I am distressed for you, my brother Jonathan; very pleasant have you been to me; your love to me was wonderful, passing the love of women" (II Sam. 1:26). One gay columnist infers that after this traumatic expe-

rience in which David's lover was murdered, he became impotent. The text for such a conclusion is Psalm 32:4, "my moisture is turned into the drought of summer."

Gay theology is, at best, an apology. Its defensive approach is geared toward self-justification for a much-maligned homophile community rather than for curious heterosexual churchmen. For this reason it need not be sophisticated nor consistent, merely impressive. And impressive it is. Verses long considered as clearly condemning homosexual behavior become vague and are reinterpreted to condone such activity. Other Scriptures conveniently disappear or are invalidated. In all, the apology is sufficient for unsophisticated gays who find comfort in the thought that David, Jesus, Paul, Ruth, and John were homosexuals. Their theology has reached its goal, despite what has happened to sound interpretation in the process.

For the gay church, all that remains is the fulfilment of the divine mandate to reach the homophile community. As Jim Sandmire (MCC-SF) words it:

> I think [MCC] is a new revelation.

> I think that the Lord has picked the most despised of his children to lead the Christian world back to an understanding of the basics of Christianity — essentially that we are to love people and that Jesus Christ died for everyone without exception.

Gay church in a straight jacket? In a theological sense perhaps, but unhindered otherwise.

4: Gaiety and the Laity

ARE YOU AVAILABLE?

I know of someone who wants to become your lover. He wants to supply you with all your needs. He wants to give you the happiest days of your life. And he asks very little in return.

Ever hear this tale before? So many times our dream man or woman is rich, has everything we could ask for and he whisks us away to live happily ever after.

Well, this "dream" can come true. There is someone who can give you all you need and more and who will love you for an eternity. And he only asks that you love him in return.

That person is Jesus Christ. He will make you happier than you have ever been in your life.

Riding the crest of its newly realized popularity, the Metropolitan Community Church has embarked on a crash evangelism and outreach effort designed to lure unconverted gays into its membership. Tracts like the one cited above, distributed in gay bars, are part of that strategy. Once unconverted gays are safely within the fold, programs are presented to satisfy the new church members. Thus on both fronts the infant denomination is beginning to form a mature organization with which to meet the needs of the community it serves. Classic evangelism, the natural outreach of a fundamentalist group such as MCC, has met with surprising success. In Phoenix, Arizona, for example, the work of an evangelism team produced the situation described in the following letter (printed in *The New Messenger*, October 1, 1972).

> Dear Chuck,
>   Last night me and Jim went bar hopping. Man did I ever have a headache when I woke up this morning, and that's not all I had with me. Do you remember that cute little blond number that you pointed out to me a couple of weeks ago?
>   Anyway, about midnight, we were in our third bar of the evening when this fat gray haired guy came in; come to find out he was a bible-thumper, belonged to Metropolitan something church. It's supposed to be a church where gay guys are welcome or something; anyway, I'm going this Sunday, just for kicks.
>
>   Lots of Luck,
>   Jim

The "fat gray haired bible-thumper" was undoubtedly roaming from bar to bar distributing tracts and leaflets about the church and soliciting attendance for Sunday's worship service. The result was that Jim probably came to MCC the next week. There is a good chance that he continued; and perhaps he even led Chuck into the fold.

The scene in Phoenix is far from unique. Across the country, wherever MCC congregations are to be found, members of evangelism teams can be seen in gay bars and restaurants sipping drinks and sharing the word that "God loves gays, too." Questions from straight Christians whether bar-hopping and witnessing are really compatible activities produce hostility among the gays. Colorado Springs columnist "Trixie" writes:

> I feel that the [charge that] MCC should not demean itself to the level of the bars is to deny the church the most logical avenue of outreach. Moreover, this attitude is typical of the beliefs of some of the established churches — the very ones who refuse to welcome us as gays to their holier-than-thou

fellowship — who tell us that it is sinful to drink or dance or play cards or go to bed with anyone for any reason other than to abet the population explosion. But MCC tells us that Jesus loves us even if we go to a gay bar (*The Catalyst*, July 30-August 13, 1972).

In San Francisco, MCC bar ministers begin their Saturday night outreach program by attending Catholic charismatic worship services and then move from bar to bar along famed Polk Street with smiles and tracts for all who are receptive. The tracts themselves, unlike the general evangelism strategy, are far from conventional. Provocative titles couched in the suggestive terminology of the gay subculture proclaim, "Try it at least once," and ask the proverbial question, "Looking for a lover?" These phrases, familiar in the homophile community, speak of the need to try MCC and to find the lover who will never leave — Jesus Christ. "What are you doing tomorrow?" one of these cleverly designed tracts reads:

> Tonight you are having a good time, but will you have a good time tomorrow and all the tomorrows after that? Tonight you might find love, but will that love be with you tomorrow? There is one way to follow that will guarantee love and happiness for all the tomorrows in your life. That way is the way of Christ. His love can give you eternal happiness. Christ loves *all* men no matter what their race or their sexual inclination.

The Mother Church goes about things a bit differently, as might be expected in a city that houses over sixty gay bars, where (it is estimated) between 10 p.m. and 2 a.m. at least a thousand men pass through the doors of one of the larger bars (Gagnon and Simon, p. 174). Invading such a bar, a group headed by Willie Smith surrounds the piano and directs the customers in an informal "sing-spiration." Soon the bar is swelling with gospel tunes and a steady flow of requests assures a lively tempo. At this point, team members individually contact customers and spread "heavenly sunshine" mingled with invitations to MCC. As quickly as they appeared, the evangelists leave, despite the entreaties of the unconverted but much-impressed gays.

Outside of the local gay bar, the largest and most heralded assembly of homosexuals may be found in the nearest federal, state, or county correctional facility. Labor leader James Hoffa, himself a prisoner for a time, once stated, according to one MCC minister, that 45% of all inmates are homosexual. Other estimates from across the nation have been as high as 85%. The Metropolitan Community Church's announcement of support for a National Director of Prison Ministry seems, on that basis, more than justified.

The Rev. Joseph Gilbert currently fills this position. Since accepting the job he has immersed himself in activity on countless fronts. Local church and district level workshops have been organized to explain the unique cruelties inflicted on gay inmates and the aid that MCC has to offer. The chief form of mistreatment is the isolation techniques that attempt to prevent gays from establishing male prostitution networks. Recently, a prison minister came across one such case in which a man had not entertained one visitor in eleven years. Under the leadership of San Diego deacon Bud Bunce, MCC has begun a letter-writing crusade to open lines of communication between free and imprisoned gays. As of this writing Gilbert's work with California prison officials has met with frustration and refusal of permission for an avowed homosexual to conduct religious services within a state institution. Gilbert, in turn, has filed a suit against the State of California and is confident of a reversal of the prohibition in the very near future. The Rev. Richard Vincent of MCC-Dallas is already successfully holding weekly services in the county jail.

Complementing the more familiar evangelism outreaches are the special ministries that the Metropolitan Community Church has developed. These programs are varied and often arise and flourish as needs in each congregation dictate. In Los Angeles special classes are offered to lesbian mothers; in Costa Mesa a burgeoning Sunday School is underway; in San Diego John Hose counsels gay Navy men who are absent without leave.

Work toward civil rights and law reform (see Chapter 8) is common, as are self-help programs designed to reduce the high unemployment rate that burdens the gay world. Growing American Youth (G.A.Y.), the denomination's youth group, has active chapters in many MCC congregations, including coffeehouse ministries in Seattle and Los Angeles. The Seattle church is also probably at the forefront in providing a special ministry to the lesbian members of the fellowship.

At its 1973 general conference, the MCC specifically singled out three groups as primary objects of concern for the following year. First was a ministry to women; that is, MCC is officially seeking to draw females into its membership. Second, the various ethnic groups were listed as a focus for ministry. Perhaps the most startling group to be named, however, were straight Christians. One of MCC's main future efforts will be to encourage straights to join and work in the gay church. Especially being sought are heterosexual ministers willing to pastor MCC flocks. At present two such men are in the wings but progress is slow, with doubt arising from both sides. For the most part, though, the ministry to the straight world will fall into educational programs that gays hope to present. At present the demand for homosexuals who will serve in this capacity exceeds their availability, but it may be assumed that the vision of gays reaching straights may eventually be realized. Says San Diego pastor John Hose, "We've the right to disseminate literature which educates the public, and it's a rare week when we're not on some college or high school campus." In their outreach to straight churches, the gay Christians have met with various degrees of success. Several denominations have abandoned age-old prohibitions to welcome the gays while others have staunchly refused and condemned the homosexuals. (This area will be discussed in detail in Chapter 6.)

In most cases, the specialized ministries are headquartered in a crisis center where gays can come without fear for counseling, suicide prevention, employment

advice, and material and financial support. The San
Francisco church is currently planning a center that
would be staffed by two psychologists (male and female),
one psychiatrist, and counselors for alcoholics and drug
addicts. In Salt Lake City (considered in the gay world
"the Closet Capital of the Midwest") the congregation is
presently working with a government agency in a mental
health pilot program, with all counselors and ministerial
staff having received professional training from the
Mental Health Department.

The Crisis Intervention Committee of MCC-LA, the
denomination's first crisis center, began quite spontane-
ously as Troy Perry found his home phone in Huntington
Park the object of countless daily calls.

> That phone number must have been the hottest in town.
> Everyone was calling. They wanted information; they wanted
> counseling. Some thought we were a call-boy service. Some
> really desperately needed help. We never hung up. We played
> it by ear, and we talked to people. One young man called one
> time and was so depressed he was planning to commit suicide.
> Well, there it was in the middle of the night. I got Wlllie
> Smith up and we drove over and talked to him. He found that
> someone cared. We helped him. And he's been an active
> member ever since (Perry, p. 146).

That midnight experience led to the formation of the
Crisis Intervention Committee. While volunteers man
the telephones 24 hours a day, others are prepared to
seek out and minister to the despairing individuals who
hope to find refuge in MCC. With an average of over
1900 calls per month, the group soon realized that its
services were inadequate. The volunteers began to em-
bark on training programs to equip themselves better for
their work. Professional counselors in drug problems
and suicide prevention offered their time and expertise.
A sympathetic professor developed a social program for
the church, while local agencies established ties with the
gay Christian group. Civil servants donated their time
and lawyers made their skills available at a minimum
fee. The Probation Department, Human Resources, and

the United States Department of Health, Education, and Welfare soon found themselves involved with this "deviant" but sincere group of men.

Yet amid the excitement of an expanding MCC ministry, there are still those who stand in unresolved despair. At least this is the opinion of John Hose, who hopes to build a retirement home for aging homosexuals in the San Diego area. He asks the question that inevitably comes to haunt every gay person: "Who's the loneliest person in the world but a sixty-year-old homosexual?" With youth and physical beauty at a premium in the gay subculture, it is truly the elderly who become the marginal members of homophile society. In Los Angeles the Mother Church is seeking to meet the needs of another handicapped group, deaf gays, by having all of their services translated into sign language. The ministry to the deaf was founded by the Rev. Richard Ploen. A former professor and dean at a Christian college, as well as missionary to Sudan, Africa, Ploen was Troy Perry's first ministerial recruit and proved to be an invaluable aid in the development of MCC. Shortly after joining he organized a Christian Education program for the infant denomination. Out of this grew the concern for deaf-mutes, and Ploen began regularly translating his fellow-minister's sermons. With impressive qualifications (Master of Christian Education and Master of Divinity degrees), his classes are considered to be outstanding. Deaf-mute teachers are continually being trained, and the program has progressed to the point that a silent choir has been formed. Hymns are shared through sign language rather than speech. Today Perry reserves the highest praise and admiration for this man, whom he labels "a solid pillar of Christianity."

By far the most impressive step into specialized outreach, however, has been in the area of ministry to blind homosexuals. Michael S. Nordstrom, 29, blind and gay, is a former Catholic Seminarian and YMCA program director. Today he is the MCC minister to the blind. Two years ago, Nordstrom underwent surgery to

correct a lifelong heart condition. Part of the treatment
included doses of a drug, which in curing his heart condition cost him his sight. Now on national tour, he
explains the handicaps of the blind and hopes to develop
MCC programs to meet their needs.

When the doctor first told Nordstrom that there was
no hope of regaining his sight, his first thoughts turned
toward suicide. In his confusion, Nordstrom crossed the
path of Troy Perry, with whom he had formerly worked
in the Mother Church. The blind minister vividly recalls
those crucial moments in his life:

> He began telling me that God cares, but I really wasn't
> listening. It seemed too easy for him to say those things. But
> then we walked in his garden. He stooped down, picked some
> flowers, and in a firm voice asked me what made me think that
> God could make flowers grow and not care about me?
> (*Advocate*, May 9, 1973).

That was the question that transformed a life, and the
response was "a ministry to the blind that I wouldn't
have been able to do if God hadn't taken away my sight.
God's taking of my sight is a positive thing. He is not a
vengeful God. He has a special work for me to do."

One of Nordstrom's efforts has been to raise funds to
make Braille copies of Perry's autobiography available
to blind homosexuals. In conjunction with this project
he is promoting an educational program that centers
around three points. First, that there *are* blind homosexuals; second, that blind people have the same drives
and desires that sighted people do ("there are teachers
of the blind that told me they thought blind people never
had sex"); third, that blind gays need to discuss their
sexuality, their blindness, and God's concern for them.

The most effective outreach of the gay church has
come by way of its publications. Yet these have also
caused some of the most serious turmoil within the fellowship. The controversy arises over the delineation of
a true definition of an MCC publication. The Mother
Church, with her unquestioned authority being examined
on a rare occasion, maintains that the purpose of a

church newsletter is primarily spiritual. MCC exists to serve God and it stands above sexuality and gayness. One MCC-LA deacon, and a member of the church's publications board, feels that every MCC piece of literature should be presentable to any straight minister with the expectation that he would be edified by a reading of the material.

The San Diego church, on the other hand, appears to operate out of the exact opposite conviction that any of its material should make a straight churchman blush. *The Prodigal,* the congregation's Christian outreach publication, is advertised as "pure, instructive, and amusing," though its pages call those adjectives into question. The Rev. Howard Williams, an editor of the publication, maintains that the magazine is designed to reach the average gay in the street in San Diego, not MCC ministers, nor gays in other geographical areas. The editors of *The Prodigal,* producing the only gay newspaper in a city with a homosexual population estimated at 75,000, feel that it is mandatory for its contents to be sufficiently provocative to interest the secular audience.

The effort to be "provocative" would seem to be more than realized. "Dr. Feelgood," the *nom-de-plume* of a local physician on the MCC-SD Personal Services Committee, has developed a controversial reputation as a result of his bi-weekly column. A recent three-part series on masturbation represented the general tenor of much of this publication. Dr. Feelgood instructed his readers about methods and techniques in addition to dispelling common false notions about masturbation. He listed what were alleged to be world records for the shortest time taken to achieve orgasm and the number of orgasms per twenty-four-hour period, and spiced the articles with quotations from Aristotle, Goethe, and Gandhi lifted out of context and twisted to create sexual implications.

It is that sort of treatment of sensitive subject matter that has led some in the MCC to dispute Pastor Hose's

claim that *The Prodigal* is an important evangelistic
device. One member from the Mother Church publicly
proclaimed that all copies of *The Prodigal* should be
gathered and burned, along with the editor. The San
Diego church also received a letter from MCC's Okla-
homa congregation, which disturbed Hose enough to
publish the following defense for the magazine:

> A somewhat less than "loving" letter came from our brothers
> and sisters in Oklahoma City lamenting about the content of
> *one* of the recent copies of the PRODIGAL. I question not
> their right to be critical — I am somewhat suspect of their
> motivation. There must be — somewhere in the great state of
> Oklahoma — some brothers and sisters who need to hear the
> word of the Lord, and some missionary effort is needed to
> bring the "Good News" to more people. . . . Although at
> times it looks like we're getting into the sty with the pigs, in
> reality, we're just following our Lord's command "Go ye
> therefore into Jerusalem and Judea, to Samaria, and even to
> the uttermost part of the earth" (*The Prodigal,* January 21,
> 1973).

Objections have not been restricted to those in the
fellowship: the church recently received a letter from
the Director, Office of Administrative Services in Los
Angeles:

> The Postal Administration of New Zealand has advised this
> office that mail which you sent was examined and found to
> contain obscene literature. For that reason it was disposed of
> in accordance with their regulations (*The Prodigal,* January 2,
> 1972).

The only response to the action was by *Prodigal* gossip
columnist "Peregrine Grape," who was flattered by the
reference to the magazine as "literature" and stated "it's
not quite as bad as being banned in Boston, but it is a
notch above being censured in Sacramento by St. Paul."

Discussion concerning MCC publication policies is
not restricted to the San Diego church, however. San
Francisco's controversial first edition of *Cross Currents*
ruffled the feathers of Rev. James Sandmire, who immediately stopped distribution of the magazine and issued
a pastoral letter to all members of the San Francisco

congregation. His three-page statement included these remarks:

> While I do not think the cover or other pictures of nudes are in any way obscene, I believe the nudity does not enhance the religious message intended, and may detract from it. Given our present state of mind, the nudity is all we see. To the extent such photography does this it is disturbing. This is not to say nudity cannot be used in religious subjects. Great artists through the centuries have used it to convey innocence and wonder at God's creation. In this issue the photographs do not, in my opinion, convey those meanings with sufficient strength to overcome the sense of unease they inspire.

In short, the publications situation is a far from settled issue. Nevertheless, it remains as the church's most potent form of outreach, whether the end result be admirable or not.

A recent development is the formation of the Good Samaritan Seminary, the first exclusively gay seminary in history. Its foundation was laid when John Hose, then associate pastor of MCC-LA, wrote a dissertation on the need for a gay seminary, for which he received the Master of Science degree in Education from the University of Southern California. Good Samaritan Seminary currently boasts an enrollment of thirty students, which, on their graduation, will nearly double the present pastoral staff for the entire denomination.

While MCC is developing internal ministries (including a National Association of Deacons), it is simultaneously expanding its denominational outreach. With an MCC congregation to be found in nearly every major American city, the church is now embarking on a more sophisticated mission program. The Rev. Lee J. Carlton, Executive Secretary of the Board of Evangelism and World Missions and Perry's successor in MCC-LA, has recently instituted a "Target Cities" program intending to set up congregations in twelve American cities per year. The first group (including Cleveland, Toledo, Columbus, Cincinnati, Louisville, Memphis, and Nashville) formed a line that fell in the middle of the nation and bisected the "Bible Belt." From this point the expectation is that the church will gradually become established in the Midwestern areas, where it is weakest. Some of the churchmen are less than optimistic about the chances of success for the Target Cities program. John Hose simply states, "I think we'll always be an urban movement because gays just can't come out in small towns."

If it appears, then, that MCC has nearly exhausted American metropolitan centers, foreign cities must seem especially inviting. It is, in fact, this front on which the gay denomination hopes to expand. Already plans are being drawn for missions in Canada, Australia and New Zealand, Great Britain, most countries in Western Europe, Japan, India, the Philippines, Malaysia, Singapore, Israel, and Latin America.

For Troy Perry, only a glimpse of his dream has materialized. For the moment he must concern himself with keeping pace with the phenomenal growth that the denomination has experienced. The pastor-turned-Moderator speaks unhesitatingly as a man with a vision:

> Now we number into the thousands of active members. We are open to all, gay and straight, black and white, and whatever. Many come to worship, some to seek faith, some to renew it, some to discover it for the first time, some to rediscover. It is never easy. From those who come, we marshal the troops for our campaigns for our rights. Those campaigns are our crusade, our mission, and we've just begun. . . . What stops us! Nothing, really. We're on our way (Perry, p. 223).

5: Lesbians, Liturgy, and Lavender Ladies

The gay church, as its very name suggests, presents a unique paradox. The sexual and spiritual areas of the gay churchmen's lives are difficult — if not impossible — to distinguish. It is not surprising, then, that a complex and unique set of problems arises. Consistency is elusive for those scouting shadowy areas in unexplored regions, and it is always the pioneer who suffers along the way. The Metropolitan Community Church, as the pioneer in homosexual religion, now finds itself in such a predicament. Faced with the problems that could only surface with the emergence of the gay church paradox, MCC now begins its task of sorting and solving questions in uncharted lands. The process of informal canonization follows with the prayer that each separate decision will somehow mesh into a coherent, noncontradictory statement on church practice.

Along with philosophical and moral questions, which unceasingly plague gay churchmen, a very practical problem is found in the areas of church procedure. The fledgling denomination is finding the unity that characterizes an oppressed minority inadequate to be the sole source of unity in a church setting. A myriad of religious backgrounds produce administrative and congregational level conflicts that force either compromise or polarization, and neither option rests easy with an adamant believer. Catholics, born and raised in exclusivism, are not quick to sacrifice that style of faith even for the new-found freedom in worship that gay religion affords. Similarly, their fundamentalist counterparts consider the pomp and ritualism of liturgical services dry and unspiritual. Thus MCC finds itself saddled with an embarrassing situation. An offer for a church where gays can worship God freely is often spurned out of traditional denominational prejudices — a problem that strikes the founding fathers of the religious body as petty at best. And yet efforts have been made, some fairly successful, to bridge the gap created by differences in style of worship.

Troy Perry once said, "We preach in so many different ways that you're bound to like some of them." There is much truth in that statement. With an estimated 40% of the MCC membership coming out of the Roman Catholic Church and an equal percentage from fundamentalist groups, no single worship service could possibly be satisfactory to the entire congregation. In some areas this problem has been approached by instituting a "take-your-pick" variety of Sunday services. In one particular case this was accomplished by offering increasingly formalized worship over the four Sundays of each month. Thus, on the first Sunday of the month the congregation could expect the spontaneity and emotional fervor of a Pentecostal prayer meeting. A week later this would be reduced to the informality of the Baptist service; the third Sunday was constructed around a more liturgical Episcopalian celebration; and the fourth Sunday was reserved for a high mass of Roman Catholic nature. In months with a fifth Sunday, the final service was an "experimental" one. The standard MCC attempt toward unity in worship involves taking elements typical of each denomination, and making the service an amalgamation of the various forms of worship. An evangelical song service might be followed by a formal procession, with traditional announcements and exhortations scattered in between.

The form of worship, however, is not unrelated to religious doctrine. And so, if there is conflict in worship style, the problems to be found at the roots are much more serious. Doctrines of apostolic succession, progressive revelation, psychic communication, and eternal salvation intermingle and clash. But it is the ageless conflict between charismatic gifts and dispensationalism that appears to be the most crucial threat to doctrinal unity. Perry's Pentecostal emphasis, although accepted by many members of the fellowship, fails to set well with some of the congregations. Renewal meetings that administer the "baptism of the Spirit" with an accompanying gift of tongues are disdained by the conservative members of the church, although manifestations of charismatic gifts are becoming more common. The San Francisco church, whose pastor is not charismatic, boasts that every one of the nine "gifts of the Spirit" is in operation in that body. Claims of healing are common, as are prophetic messages and the devotional use of praying in tongues. The pastor of the Seattle church, Robert Sirico, was once the leader of the Charismatic Renewal Movement in that city. He called a press conference to confess that he was homosexual, that he liked the way he was, that God had made him gay, and that prayers for his healing were wrongly directed because he was not living in sin. Now the man who used to advertise: "Don't miss the healing services of Robert Sirico, a Spirit-filled man blessed by God" is busy infusing his congregation with that same spirit. Sister churches are not as sympathetic. John Hose of San Diego dismisses the charismatic experience as an "emotional appeal" that will fade, while MCC-Denver pastor Bob Darst can describe the movement as no more than a "pagan custom."

Besides worship and doctrine, other differences trouble the church's dream for peaceful waters. Regional differences hinder the fellowship from becoming a single voice in the nationwide gay community. Los Angeles gays

enjoy favorable publicity and MCC-Hawaiians find increased sexual liberty, but Atlanta members struggle
against Southern prejudice, and Boston's congregation
faces classic conservatism. The West is free, the East is
formal, and MCC's General Conference inherits the problems of each. More complex problems also arise because
the gay members themselves are primarily conservative,
both politically and religiously, and thus they are not the
pliable tools for social change with which MCC pastors
expected to work. And although MCC congregations are
located in urban settings where gays can emerge from
closets without fear of reprisal, they must suffer the con-
sequences of an inner-city existence. Finally, with youth
at a premium in the gay world, the youth group of the
fellowship must always be on guard for solicitations. As
a member of one congregation put it, in speaking about
their youth group, "The Chicken Coop," "our biggest
problem is watching out for chicken hawks."

Viewed through the eyes of the straight world, gay
Christianity perhaps reaches the peak of inconsistency in
its ethics. There is no doubt that MCC struggles with this
problem. Given the gay theologians' handling — or dis-
carding — of the Scriptures, the gay church has dif-
ficulty finding something to rely on as a standard for moral
behavior. The question to be decided is whether to accept traditional fundamentalistic morals (minus the homosexual prohibitions) or to abandon them completely in
favor of a new homosexual ethic.

Along the former path, familiar elements of the gay
life-style can be seen as incompatible with Christianity.
"The baths" and "tearoom trade" are two such examples.
The baths, in the gay world, are primarily establishments
where rooms and partners are for rent. Sex is impersonal,
noncommittal, and readily available. San Francisco's
Gay Church of God minister Ray Broshears comments
on the baths:

> I was taken on a tour of one once and all I could see in there
> was one mass fantastic orgy. Which is wrong. I think sex is a
> very personal thing. Public sex is wrong, group sex is wrong.

Across town, James Sandmire displays a less restrictive view:

> Paul talks about the freedom of the man who lives in the Spirit. I can't tell you what is wrong. I don't care if you go to the baths. You decide that. If you have the Spirit you are liberated, you can go to the baths, because you don't *have* to go. If you *have* to go home with him, or you *have* to go to the baths, then you are a slave. That is wrong, that is sin.

> If you have gone to bed together and have both decided that that is what you wanted to do; if you have touched one another and your lives are better for it, and you don't feel bad about it, then you can be sure you're right.

The "tearoom trade" refers to the homosexual activity that commonly takes place in public rest rooms. Again, impersonality is the key feature of such a relationship, and the motives are purely hedonistic. MCC-Costa Mesa pastor Rodger Harrison asks the question:

> Now what do you do with tea room queens? I just draw the line. Sex in public is disgusting, and the MCC Church is one of the few positive forces in the gay world saying, "Stay out of the tearooms. Why embarrass straight people?"

Pornography is a similar issue. The struggle against the availability of pornographic and erotic material has long been associated with the Christian church, especially its conservative branches. At this point, the gay church is trapped in an uncomfortable situation. The homosexual life-style easily accommodates pornographic literature. How ought gay Christians to react? We have mentioned earlier some of the incongruities in the congregational newsletters of the Metropolitan Community Church, and the extent of this is indeed startling. Pages filled with articles of praise to God are followed by columns that discuss sexual intimacies; a picture of Christ stands alongside an advertisement for "Diablo's: San Diego's Sin Spot." Equally amazing is the practice of MCC congregations distributing secular gay magazines among its members. In many churches such publications rest alongside Bible Study guides and devotional materials.

It is evident that the heterosexual moral standard is

being subtly replaced. Sandmire, indeed, believes this to be a necessity. He feels that there are some basic Christian rules regarding sexual relationships — principally that a person should never be used.

> You must never use another person as a receptacle for your semen. You must truly seek relationships — now that can be a one night stand. The minute you view a person as a simple object to gratify your own desires, you commit sexual sin. Gays are going to have to come up with their own definition of a Christian sexual ethic.

Douglas Dean, editor of MCC *Cross Currents* and author of several erotic paperbacks (the latest, *Gay Mexico,* advertised as "a breezy and witty guide to the 'in' spots south of the border illustrated with photos of the author's young Mexican friends") echoes Sandmire's views.

> There is no reason, after all, while we endeavor to form some standards of ethical conduct among ourselves in our gay communities, that we must copy the standards of heterosexuals. We all know that heterosexuals do not abide by their own declared standards, anyway.

> We Gays pride ourselves on our honesty. As we liberate ourselves from the false standards of a heterosexual society, why can't we establish ethics of our own, ethics which are not based on lies and hypocrisy but on the truth as we know it (*Cross Currents,* Fall 1972).

One of the tenets of the Metropolitan Community Church is that services are open to all. No individual will be excluded on the basis of race, creed, or sexual orientation. Here the fellowship finds itself in an uncomfortable situation. Having opened the door to themselves as homosexuals, they find it more difficult to remain open for the subcultures that deviate from the gay life-style. With some embarrassment the church is attempting to delineate a stand regarding "drag queens" or transvestites (males who dress as females and gain pleasure from the acting out of sexual fantasies), the "leather set" (gay males who emphasize ultra-masculinity), and sadomasochists (individuals who derive sexual excitement by inflicting or enduring physical pain and torture). The dilemma is that if MCC excludes these groups from their congregation, the bases of their arguments for the existence of their church are weakened. But the presence of these groups proves to be a source of embarrassment before the critical eyes of the straight church which is judging MCC's legitimacy.

The attitude of a drag queen is expressed by a writer in the Dallas' church newsletter:

> When I come to MCC I want to be myself and dress like I feel. MCC is supposed to be open to everyone as they are. If I can't come in drag and be welcome, then I feel the Church is being hypocritical and that is why I don't go to other churches.

> I know that some people are embarrassed when I wear drag but do I have to stop being myself so they won't be upset? It's hard enough being hassled at work and harassed on the streets. Isn't there somewhere we can go and be accepted just as we are? (*The Channel*, January 7, 1973).

The article continues to implore those who are against drag not to judge another by outward appearance and to advise transvestites to dress out of a natural feeling rather than to put on a show. They are instructed to wear clothing that would not offend others and to strive to make all their actions natural and not overly effeminate. This reaction is common to the gay church. The Rev. Rodger Harrison, who has ministered to transvestites in his Orange County, California, congregation, discusses the situation a bit more bluntly:

> A drag queen is a fetish, and although I don't understand it, I support the right of the drag queen to have his particular fetish. I think the church should be elastic enough to make provisions for drag queens to live out this fetish. It doesn't hurt; it's a crime without a victim. What I am saying is that the [straight] church has got to swing around to the point that a drag will come to church in high heels and would be accepted as a child of God for whom Christ died. But I would hope that she would be tactful enough to underemphasize her femininity, his femininity. Underdo the make-up a little bit.

Only 4% of all transvestites are gay; the remainder are

heterosexual men who, except for their desire to dress like females, are no different from the rest of male society. Harrison believes therefore that one of the ministries of MCC is to reach out to these straight transvestites who would be shunned by their own churches, yet accepted by gays.

One method used to alleviate pressure in this area by several of the MCC congregations is the establishment of a church club that is a society of transvestites called the "Lavender Ladies." Here they are able to act in drama productions that are performed before the entire congregation. Both camps are satisfied and there is no room for embarrassment. Masquerade balls and Halloween parties are also classic methods of releasing drag queens for an evening. Perhaps though, the wearing of drag is not confined simply to a small minority. The May Festival of 1970, one of MCC's banquets, was described as having been patronized by 300 homosexual Christians, with males dressed in "silk, taffeta, high heels, and extravagant coiffures and gay girls in formal, masculine evening attire" (*Advocate,* June 10, 1970).

The leather set stands in direct opposition to transvestism. Living in a world of ultra-masculinity, these gays heighten every feature of maleness in order to attract potential partners. The "leather" name is derived from the attire of this subculture, which principally consists of leather jackets, pants, and boots, with chains. Motorcycles are commonly used for transportation. Leather bars have certain unwritten rules that distinguish them from other bars. No effeminate behavior is tolerated, and dancing and outward signs of affection are, if not prohibited, strongly discouraged. Another point of difference is that the leather set is often connected with sadomasochistic activity which hardly qualifies for the "crime without a victim" classification sometimes used for homosexuality in general. Sadomasochistic (known as S/M) homosexuals are frightening to many gays, who are afraid of being lured unsuspectingly to a home where they will be beaten and tortured. Since there is no way to identity sadists beforehand, gays may take their lives in their hands when becoming involved with such an individual. A typical ad by a sadist that was run in the *Advocate* reads:

M's WANTED

by young cattle baron. Must be sexy, freaky, hearty and not a beginner. Have playhouse, with rack, have barn, have dungeon. If you need to be corraled and trained, used and abused, answer this ad and it will happen.

Specific rules guard the "game," and it is normally established in advance to what extent the torture will run. Most S/M gays wear keys hanging from their belts to indicate their role preference — keys on the right side indicate a preference for masochism, keys on the left advertise sadistic tendencies. Gloves and chains are similar indicators.

Despite the horror that the S/M scene often produces, the Metropolitan Community Church has sought —with some hesitation — to draw them into the fold. "Bill Q." of MCC-Denver, in an article entitled "Leather Mystique," enumerates the positive points of S/M society: their bars are friendlier to those on the inner circle, the atmosphere is nonjudgmental, people are more frank about sexual tastes, age is of less importance, their sexuality is "expressive" and uninhibited, sex is based on a greater degree of trust and tenderness, love grows from the commitment made to one another. His closing paragraphs deride the prejudice of the church and gay community for blocking the acceptance of leather and S/M gays.

We must demand an end to discriminatory treatment. When the closet door swings open, it opens for everyone. Liberation is not just for the gay people whom society finds it easiest to accept; it is for all of us. There can be no such thing as a second class homosexual, somebody who is expected to remain in the closet while more acceptable gays take their place in society (*The Catalyst*, May 20, 1973).

Sandmire made a first step in this direction of acceptance by conducting a "leather mass," but others are considerably more cautious when dealing with this mysterious group. A few MCC pastors, while accepting the leather set, totally turn from any approval of sadomasochistic sexual activity. Rodger Harrison is one:

> Sadomasochism, for me, falls in the category of illness. I really don't have much sympathy for them. Sadomasochism is almost psychopathic. I'm not sure whether you're talking about chains, whips, and so forth . . . but it's a very dangerous homosexual activity. I feel the person in this bizarre spectrum needs a psychiatrist.

Another problem unknown to straight churches, but prevalent in the gay church, is an inherent antagonism between the male and female members of the congregation, or as one individual phrased it, "gay girls just don't like gay boys." In heterosexual churches, male-female bonds often form the backbone for operation of church programs. In the gay world, however, the same-sex orientation and the gap between sexes seem firmly entrenched.

On the other hand, Phyllis Lyon of the San Francisco-based National Sex Forum, a leading champion of the lesbian-feminist movement, who estimates that there are probably seventeen million lesbians in the United States, is astounded by the activity of women in the gay church. Although the female membership in MCC is no higher than 10% of the total congregation, Lyon finds even that percentage incredible, for she feels gay men are just as chauvinistic as straight men. About MCC she comments:

> The church is a male organization and there really is no place for women. It is beyond me why there are any women involved at all in the churches. I can't understand why they haven't all walked out.

Sandmire, whose congregation formerly retained female associate minister Alice Naumoff before she departed over "personal differences," agrees with Lyon in many respects. He feels that the church, founded by men, has paid more attention toward the male membership, but he excuses this situation as characteristic of the entire gay world. Sandmire suggests that all the blame need not rest with the men. The women find themselves having to choose between the gay liberation and women's liberation movements as to which their enthusiasm and loyalty should be dedicated. At present the latter is more in vogue, which irritates impatient gay churchmen, who are eager to get their denomination stabilized. Thus, it appears that turbulent waters may be ahead. The San Francisco church has already had to do some rethinking on this score: the title of its newsletter, "Speaking-Up: the Voice of Gay Men," drew charges of sexism and the offensive phrase was dropped.

While many, such as Phyllis Lyon, can see no future for women in the gay church, others are willing to challenge the discriminatory attitudes of the fellowship from within the walls. Licensed MCC minister Freda Smith of Sacramento is one. In fact, she is optimistic enough to consider the Metropolitan Community Church "the vanguard of the Christian feminist movement." In explaining the unique sexual roles within the church (men without wives at home serving as unpaid housekeepers, women without husbands who would view them as burdens), Smith outlines the key position of MCC in the movement.

> The way will be led by the one church in which the sexes are not dependent on oppressing each other. In no other church in the world, at this time, are men and women so capable of looking at each other as human beings and not as extensions to the roles society has insisted they adopt (*Cross Currents*, Spring 1973).

Given the denomination's "affirmative action" toward women, there appears to be some degree of hope for reconciliation. In San Jose, where MCC's Northwest Regional District held a recent conference, a lesbian caucus convened and established three formal recommendations to the fellowship: (1) that MCC publish articles on women and the Bible and that a full-scale effort be made to recruit more women; (2) that female deacons be given a uniform, so that their position may be visible to other women; and (3) that special classes be added to the seminary curriculum to prepare women for the ministry. In the Seattle church, where there is a sizable number of Christian lesbians, the problems seem to have been solved, and thus the feminists have an example around which to build their hopes. No longer will the women of MCC accept the bondage of Pauline Christianity and resign themselves to silence in the churches.

Perhaps the aspect of the gay church that has received the most publicity has been homosexual marriage. To most straights it stands out as a curious by-product of the movement and serves as the object of anti-homosexual jokes and mockery. The gay Christians contend, however, that it is a very serious covenant, and a great deal of discussion has been afforded the subject. The very existence of gay marriage has brought previously acceptable homosexual activity into an uncomfortable light. Is sexual exclusivity really necessary? Is there a place for free love in homosexual religion? Should procedure for annulment and divorce be instituted? Courting, dating, coupling (collectively known as "cruising") — are they compatible with or essential to happiness in the gay church? Such questions erode untested church doctrines and allow self-proclaimed philosophers and theologians the opportunity to formulate hastily developed opinions.

The gay life-style is not gay. It is a genuine loneliness that enshrouds and burdens those within its walls. The search for a dream lover forms the daily pilgrimage of most homosexuals. Despite apologies for cruising ("we care enough to take the risk of sharing ourselves with others") and articles listing the advantages of being single ("being single enables one to enjoy whatever spurs him on at the moment"), there is nevertheless a continuing hope of establishing a stable relationship that will forever end the search. The editor of the MCC-Dallas newsletter, who describes himself as "young, handsome, and single," captures the loneliness that, like a thread, winds through his life.

> You know as well as I the pain of coming home to an empty room and falling into bed alone for the umpteenth time in a row. That hollow ache that the doctor wouldn't be able to find hits me after seeing happy couples or watching a duo in the movies walk happily arm in arm into the sunset (*The Channel*, February 4, 1973).

San Diego columnist Charles David realizes this all too well, but he is concerned that gays will marry for negative reasons and thus destroy the function for which the ordinance was instituted. That is, if it is merely the pressure of wanting stability and fearing loneliness that creates a couple, the church would do better to revert to the promiscuous life-style of the secular world. David demands that MCC should be "consciously, firmly and consistently supporting every social form that promotes courtship and tends to make more difficult the rush to spouseship." He considers the development of the institutions of courtship and engagement to be the primary tasks of the church at this time and advises against the MCC tradition of communion rail coupling, which romanticizes a relationship. In an article entitled "Free Love," he describes the pressures and problems of the homosexual who hopes to find stability in another man.

> All of our emotional training tells us to find a mate, a spouse, a one-to-one relationship. Rejected and afraid we rush into such relationships. We dare not, most of us, take the time to court, to learn of each other. Anyway, we have so few places to mix socially in an atmosphere productive of healthy emotional outlook. We are justifiably afraid to appear hand-in-hand in the streets, in the park . . . even in a car. We cannot risk showing any affection at theaters, restaurants, or beaches. In our own bars (healthy atmosphere?), we are not permitted to dance close in most cities (*The Prodigal*, January 2, 1973).

The gay marriage (or, as it is phrased in the Metropolitan Community Church, "Holy Union") seems to be the panacea for such ever-present problems and the end to which most gay Christians will strive.

The Holy Union is becoming extremely popular. Troy Perry alone has officiated at more than 250 unions since the founding of the church. The majority of MCC ministers now live in Holy Union (only one pastor, a bisexual, currently has a wife). Such marriages have been publicized nationwide whenever discovered. The most famous in the gay community was the union of Perry and Roller Derby star Steve Jordan. Rings are traditionally exchanged in all Holy Unions, but no one is given in marriage. In one particular instance, however, both parties in a lesbian marriage were escorted down the aisle by their fathers. "He was so proud," one of them said later, "that we all thought he would pop his buttons." A passionate kiss usually follows the vows, along with many tears. At the reception for the newly-weds it is not uncommon that the top of the wedding cake be adorned by two male figurines.

The ceremony itself is very solemn. Based on the standard service for heterosexual marriages, the words take on a new significance when applied to the homo-sexual situation.

> Good people we have come together in the presence of God to witness and proclaim the joining together of these men in Holy Union. This bond was established by God at creation, and our Lord Jesus Christ himself adorned this manner of life by his presence and first miracle at a wedding in Cana of Gal-ilee. It signifies to us the union of Christ and his Church, and Holy Scripture commends it to be honored among all men. The union of these men in heart, body, and mind is intended by God for their mutual joy.

Each member of the couple is then asked if he will take his lover "to be his man, to live together in Holy Union." He is instructed to love, comfort, honor, and keep him, in sickness and in health, to forsake all others and to be faithful to him "as long as your love shall last" (re-placing "till death do you part"). After the vows have been made, the pastor, by "the ordinance of God," pronounces that the two men are joined in Holy Union. As the couple is presented to the congregation, the minister proclaims, "Those whom God hath joined together let all men respect." The traditional hetero-sexual wording "Let no man put asunder" is not particularly compatible with the promiscuous gay life-style.

Jim Sandmire argues that the Holy Union is a unique institution that has arisen to meet a growing need in the homophile community. He unequivocally states that

> Holy Unions are *not* gay copies of heterosexual marriages. Rather they are special services in which two partners make binding lifetime commitments to one another before God and their brothers and sisters.

Having joined in marriage as many as four couples in a single day, Sandmire nevertheless prides himself on the fact that it is not easy for a couple to step into Holy Union. For him it is not something to be taken lightly. He requires, without exception, that before a couple are joined they must live together for a six-month period (a special pastoral blessing on a relationship is available for a three-month commitment), attend eight counseling classes, and attend at least one worship service at MCC, "so they can understand the seriousness with which we view our relationships with one another." For Sandmire, though, the primary requirement is that each partner understand exactly what the relationship represents to his lover, especially in regard to sexual fidelity.

> I don't care what they do, I just want them to agree upon it. You're either going to be faithful completely (and that means if you have sex with anyone else it's sin), or you're going to be faithful but occasionally you might go out, or you're going to live a reasonably promiscuous life. You know it's going to happen and it's not going to be that big of a hang-up. But if a person truly feels that he should not have sex with anyone but his lover, as far as I'm concerned, he's committing adultery if he does.

Fidelity, in other words, means honesty rather than exclusivity. Should one of the partners desire to dissolve their relationship, however, a "Release from Vows" may be issued after prayer and counseling.

In the eyes of other gays, such legalism is merely "playing church" with heterosexual rules. *Cross Currents* editor Douglas Dean speaks frankly about fidelity in the gay world.

> Let's be honest. A certain amount of sexual freedom (call it promiscuity, if you must) is a recognized part of the gay life-style. Perhaps more with the guys than the girls, but Gays are attracted to new people and on the lookout for new experiences, and a wedding ring on the finger is not (again, let's be honest!) going to stop most of us from popping into bed with somebody new who turns us on (*Cross Currents*, Fall 1972).

Robert Anderson, in a 1969 speech to the Council on Religion and the Homosexual, scoffs at the idealistic bonds that supposedly maintain a marital relationship. Although he has personally been married "gayly and happily" for over thirteen years, Anderson reduces the essence of gay marriage to one succinct point.

> Let's face it, it isn't lofty ideals of the relationship that makes the marriage go. It's the fact that love conquers all! When you're turned on to a guy, and having sex, and sex is great, and feels good, you're willing to put up with a lot and overlook a lot. Sex can get you through the rough spots. After all, in the relationship, your mind is not on that vine-covered cottage as much as in that other guy's pants (and hopefully more than your mind is there) ("Gay Marriage Between Two Males").

For the Metropolitan Community Church, the issue of gay marriages is far from settled. In its wake, though, has come a confusion of roles that will forever leave its mark on the gay world. Concepts of husbands, wives, lovers, and parents all fade into a meaninglessness, while the individuals involved beg for definitions. In Sandmire's life, the confusion became clear when his young son by a previous heterosexual marriage came running up to his lover Jack, screaming "Mommy! Mommy!" In the Sandmire home, Jack is the "mother" as far as the children are concerned, about whom the San Francisco pastor says "they don't know about me yet . . . but they are guessing."

6: The Many Faces of Gay Religion

Not all gay Christians have been content to resign themselves to a specifically homosexual denomination. Perhaps feeling that such a move is a compromise in the struggle to liberate straight Christianity, some gays have rejoined or continued their battle for acceptance by and integration into mainline denominations. Various American denominations have felt the impact of the new boldness that homosexual Christians have been recently displaying. In this decade it will not be uncommon to hear of a gay caucus at the national convention of every major church body. For many, the Metropolitan Community Church represents less than the full freedom that is being demanded. The church realizes this and as a result often encourages outreach to established denominations. Other gays, however, refuse to be patronized and, in a counter-move, openly reject MCC and its withdrawal tactics. This disparity is often a product of irreconcilable theological and political differences. Despite their boast of great followings, such groups can seldom substantiate their claims. Relegated to the plane of simply being a dissident voice, they nevertheless constitute some of the many faces of gay religion.

Although it is shocking to some, it is quite common in recent years for groups within major denominations to claim publicly that they have always been homosexual and are no longer ashamed of it. Furthermore, they are demanding acceptance in their respective religious communities. This has forced conservative churchmen across the nation to reexamine doctrines that have stood unchallenged for centuries. The Church of the Latter Day Saints, for example, has begun to notice some defections. Jim Sandmire, once a Mormon missionary and a highly respected young officer in the church, renounced his affiliations with the church after "coming out" as a homosexual. Similarly in Salt Lake City, the Metropolitan Community Church is finding its greatest outreach in a ministry to ex-Mormons. Apart from MCC, there is an active group of gay Mormons in North Hollywood known as the "Open Circle." The Society of Friends, on the other hand, apparently on the assumption that some of their members were homosexual, adopted and published "Toward a Quaker View of Sex," a document that urges full acceptance of homosexual behavior.

Other ventures into the world of straight denominations have proved less successful. Pentecostal sects, which have produced a sizable number of MCC pastors, appeared to be fertile soil for gay educational purposes, and many newly liberated homosexuals have returned to familiar charismatic prayer meetings only to find that their message, "God is for Gays," is not acceptable. In fact, several have now gone back to their original charismatic groups with prayers for their healing being offered along the way. This in turn has led, in San Francisco at least, to counter-prayers for individuals "who have fallen into the bondage of the teaching of the straight Christian world," despite the fact that some claim to have been "delivered" from their homosexuality.

Similarly, the United Methodist Church was expected to be at the vanguard of homosexual liberation. With the denomination having opened several of its church's facilities to gay congregations, there was much hope that an affirmative statement might be issued at the national level. When the 1972 quadrennial convention of the General Conference of the church was called to order in Atlanta there was a gay caucus eager to make some bold moves. They had prepared demands that would institute the ordination of homosexuals, gay sex education courses, provisions in the social creed for gays, and marriages for homosexuals. These proposals, however, were defeated; and to the amazement of the gay community, the Methodist Church stated as a matter of policy that homosexuality is "incompatible with Christian teaching." The knowledge that the denomination had previously defrocked two of its ministers who had confessed a homosexual orientation, combined with the ratification of the Conference statement by over 1,000 delegates, led the gay churchmen to comment disparagingly, "The church is regressing." Gay Methodists have, however, been able to enjoy one final note of victory. *motive,* the Methodist Student magazine, closed its publication doors by distributing two 64-page issues covering the lesbian and gay male experiences. The twin issues represented the previously unknown boldness of gay Christians but likewise stood as a symbol of the ultimate power of the straight church — *motive* no longer exists.

It was William Reagan Johnson who became the first avowed homosexual to be ordained by a major denomination, the United Church of Christ. The 26-year-old Houston native, a graduate of the Pacific School of Religion in Berkeley, California, declared his own homosexuality at a seminary symposium on the subject while in his senior year. The day was November 11, 1970, and it marked the beginning of Johnson's struggle for ordination. His ordination request was originally rejected by both the ministry committee of the Northern California Conference (UCC) and the credentials committee of the Golden Gate Association, but an appeal to the people kept his hopes and chances alive. The result was a year-long investigation of Johnson by the

United Church of Christ. On April 30, 1972, Johnson's ecclesiastical council met to decide his fate. Several hundred delegates and guests crowded into the San Carlos Community Church to view the man who was challenging church doctrine and the security it affords. After four hours of questioning about Johnson's gay life-style, letters of support were read along with the candidate's own paper, "My Pilgrimage of Faith." The historic vote was 62 to 34 in favor of ordination. According to a reporter, "the church erupted into wild spontaneous applause that lasted several minutes." Johnson simultaneously closed his eyes in thanksgiving, and with clasped hands prayed silently. At the same time a nearby UCC minister stood and announced, "This is an effrontery to Christianity!" and quickly exited. On June 25, Johnson took his vows of ordination — the date coincidentally marking the fifteenth anniversary of the denomination as well as the third commemoration of the "Stonewall rebellion," generally regarded as the beginning of the gay liberation movement.

Johnson's ordination set the precedent that many gay Christians had been seeking; they will now follow in his footsteps. He calls for homosexuals to stay in their churches and make their presence known, believing that true acceptance of homosexuality can best be effected at local rather than national levels. Although Johnson's victory was a high point in the gay liberation movement, it nevertheless kindled some mixed feelings among MCC's church officers. For the first time, the church's unchecked enthusiasm was dampened with the realization that there might not be the need for a gay denomination. Prior to the final vote, Troy Perry expressed pessimism to Johnson regarding his hopes for ordination. The moderator also offered to personally send the seminary scholar to any congregation of his choice if he was willing to become an MCC minister, with his ordination coming from the fellowship itself. Although he greatly respects the church and the offer, Johnson declined saying,

> I couldn't see failing to give the United Church the opportunity
> to respond to the concerns and needs of gay people and minis-
> ters who were gay, by simply walking away and going to MCC.

Bill Johnson's victory opened the door for reconsid-
eration by other denominations. The first was the Unitarian-Universalist Association. The Rev. Richard Nash,
37, a graduate of the University of Chicago Divinity
School, recently received unanimous approval for his
request to establish a ministry to homosexuals. In naming
him a "specialized minister for gay concerns," the denomination stated that it recognized a need "for greater
sensitivity toward and affirmation of gay people as well
as the need on the part of gay people for the services
rendered by a liberal minister." (Nash had originally
asked for the title "specialized minister for gay affairs,"
but the board recoiled at the pun.) A perhaps surprising
dimension to the Nash appointment is that he is currently
being tried on a prostitution charge. Nash's first trial
ended in a hung jury; a second trial in January 1971
produced a conviction, but eleven months later that
decision was reversed by an appeals court on grounds of
misconduct by the prosecutor. The city of Los Angeles
is trying him a fourth time at present.

Gay acceptance in liberal denominations such as the
United Church of Christ and the Unitarian-Universalist
Association is not surprising to most heterosexual Christians. One gay minister, however, is attempting what
appears to be an incredible task. The Rev. Rodger
Harrison, pastor of MCC's Costa Mesa congregation, has
petitioned the American Baptist Convention to accept
the Costa Mesa church on a dual alignment basis. The
request is now being reviewed by the Convention, while
the gay minister is encouraging support by conducting
gay sensitivity sessions in key Baptist churches. The ABC
flew Harrison to Philadelphia, where he spoke to a
collective of military chaplains on homosexuality and
the Bible. From there he went to the national head-
quarters in Valley Forge, Pennsylvania, to conduct a

conference on homosexuality and the American Baptist's responsibility.

If any avowed homosexual can surmount the fundamental background of the Baptist church, it will probably be Harrison. Intelligent, articulate and sincere, he carries all the credentials necessary to impress Convention leaders. Once a highly respected minister in ABC circles, Harrison represented the Baptists for the National Council of Churches as the Protestant chaplain to the United States and British embassies in Moscow. While there, he voluntarily made evangelistic outreaches into Moscow University, eventually gathering a respectable group of followers. Not until he had spent six years in Europe and had found a lover did Harrison return. Once in America, however, he discovered that he was in a unique situation. Assuming him to be heterosexual, the State Department's security force began questioning him as to the extent of homosexuality among Soviet military and state officials. This triggered his thinking about his own sexuality, resulting in the decision to take a pastoral position in MCC offered by Troy Perry. At the same time he was appointed as campus chaplain at Long Beach State College and the University of California at Irvine, with funds coming from the ABC. Eventually, the Director of Campus Ministries was informed of his MCC affiliation. He asked Harrison for a denial, but found him gay and proud instead. A resignation was called for, and refused. Instead of instituting dismissal procedures, the ABC withdrew his funds, expecting this to settle the situation. But Harrison continued to claim that he was an American Baptist chaplain despite the absence of financial support. The ABC was powerless and embarrassed, and the gay minister was advertising his Baptist ties with glee. He announced that to the entire ABC in Denver in 1972, and followed this with a gay caucus at Lincoln in 1973. At this writing the Baptists are still discussing their dilemma with the obvious hope of discovering a face-saving escape.

Despite their opposition on many issues, Baptists and

Roman Catholics stand solidly united in their anti-gay attitude. It is from these two groups that most gay Christians emerge; and a homosexual Catholic group, similar to the Protestant ones previously discussed, has arisen. "Dignity," a national organization of gay Roman Catholics, is probably the most articulate and organized body in gay religion. Boasting a membership of over five hundred after only two years of existence, it has chapters in a dozen cities. Dignity has three major objectives: to demonstrate that it is possible for Catholics to be both gay and Christian; to work within the Church to redevelop its theology of sex; and to correct injustices within the Church and society. Founded by an Augustinian priest/artist/psychotherapist, the organization found itself immediately burdened by guilt-ridden Catholics who sought the solace that the group advertised. American bishops were notified of the formation of Dignity, but no action against the homosexuals has been recommended or taken. In fact, in Chicago weekly gay masses are celebrated with the knowledge of the Archbishop (who simply asked that the meetings not be overly publicized), and in Los Angeles a similar situation exists under the careful eye of Cardinal Manning.

The success of these two chapters has planted a vision in the minds of many homosexual Catholics — a dream of a gay parish.

> The establishment of gay parishes where numbers would warrant it, has many advantages. The whole parish effort could be directed to the gay person. In the confessional, he would be understood. . . . The day may come when gays are tolerated in a parish, if not fully understood. But there will always be a gay lifestyle, a gay mystique. For that reason, it is this editor's opinion there will always be a need for gay parishes (*The Gay Christian*, January/February 1973).

Already there is a sizable number of priests who have "come out" as homosexuals, and given the estimate that five percent of Catholic clergy are gay, the vision of a gay parish may be realized. Once again this calls into question MCC's segregationist approach. Should gay parishes become a live option, Perry's church would probably lose half of its membership. A Dignity leader in San Diego believes that MCC only offers a social arena to gay Catholics. Although (by his figures) 95% of the membership of MCC-San Diego is Roman Catholic, he implies that many have sacrificed their faith to make contacts in the Protestant denomination. Thus the spiritual aspect of the church has no place in the lives of many of the members.

> MCC for the majority of the Roman Catholics doesn't provide a religious or theological atmosphere. The main reason that people are attending MCC is for the social atmosphere. They can make contacts, develop friendships, and so forth. I don't need to tell you that promiscuity is very frequent in the gay community. . . . The Roman Catholics are also attending masses in their parishes every Sunday.

The charge is a serious one, which challenges much of the spirituality in which the Metropolitan Community Church glories. It reduces MCC to nothing more than a cruising center, an allegation long made by secular gays.

An interesting development in the realm of gay activity in straight religious fellowships is the advent of the Metropolitan Community Temple (MCT) — the nation's first homosexual synagogue. Known technically as Beth Chayim Chadashim (House of New Life), the temple began when only four people showed up for one of MCC's Wednesday discussion meetings in April 1972. Coincidentally, all four were Jewish, which led Troy Perry to contact Rabbi Erwin Herman, director of the district's Union of American Hebrew Congregations (UAHC). Herman immediately helped the young congregation with its worship services, obtained speakers, acquired a Torah, and developed an adult education program. Within six months the attendance had risen to a high of 175, and plans were made to apply for membership in UAHC. The Gay Jews, with 40% of their congregation female, currently meet in a Reform Temple near the UCLA campus and are desperately seeking homosexual rabbis to supply leadership. Another gay Jewish group is Chutzpah (Hebrew meaning "insolence" or "impudence") in Berkeley, California.

Somewhere between those working at changing attitudes in straight churches and those dedicating themselves to the gay denomination represented by MCC, stand a group of people dedicated to gay Christianity according to their own revelation. For the most part these men are shunned by the more established homosexual churchmen. The Rt. Rev. Robert M. Clement, curial administrator of the American Orthodox church and pastor of the Church of the Beloved Disciple in New York City, is assumed to have started the first gay church. His services are basically high masses, which have attracted up to 300 worshippers. A well-known figure in the gay community, he is looked on by the MCC community as a troublemaker who is creating unrest for the New York congregation. Rev. John Hose says of Clement, "He thinks New York isn't big enough for two churches . . . we think it's big enough for 20 churches." In an effort to work some reconciliation, Troy Perry agreed to officiate at the Holy Union of Clement and his lover of twelve years, John Nolle, but the New York pastor is successful in his autonomous role and apparently will not be lured into the MCC. His advertisement for the Church of the Beloved Disciple still reads, "Gay People of New York, This is YOUR Church" — a statement that rests uncomfortably with the Rev. Howard Wells of MCC-NY.

Perhaps the purest isolationist in the entire movement is the Rev. Raymond Broshears, who claims to be the leader of San Francisco gays, an opinion not widely shared. Presiding Bishop of the Orthodox Episcopal Churches of God, Broshears, a former member of Billy James Hargis' Christian Crusade, is a dedicated social activist and is known in the area as "the Tenderloin street minister." Indeed, he has been considerably effective in meeting the needs of the minority members in the district. He has long been a social and legal advocate for the elderly, recently presenting them with $600 in food certificates as well as over $300 in gifts and supplies. The former Pentecostal pastor is currently managing a Community Center from which he conducts demonstrations against Pacific Telephone (he "crucified" one of his team members to a telephone pole in front of their employment offices), area taxi-cab companies (he threatened to smash the windows of cabs if any gay drivers were dismissed), and the Police Department ("In Germany they called them the Brownshirts, in Italy they called them the Blackshirts, and in San Francisco we call them the Bluecoats"). Broshears' church emanates from the Lithuanian Independent Catholic Church of North and South America, believes in assimilating the best truths of every religion, and is psychic-spiritualist in nature. He has successfully aligned himself with the poor and is incensed by gay churches that cater to the middle class. Broshears, who resembles the MCC moderator in his Southern manner, nevertheless reserves his most potent venom for Troy Perry:

> He drinks; that is wrong. He smokes; that is definitely wrong. He is on a very big money trip and that is very definitely wrong. He does not relate to the poor gay in any way, shape, or form. But he's made a mint off the church. He and dear old mother Perry, they're just having a ball. He really turns me off. I mean the man doesn't even resemble a human being any more . . . he's so commercial. Troy Perry is just another capitalist, rip-off pig!

Broshears feels that MCC was formed on a sexist basis and is invalid for that reason alone, a point also maintained by Bill Johnson. Furthermore, he disdains the lack of theological training in MCC, and offers his opinion that in order to be named as a pastor, "you just have to be a good queer with a lot of money or a lot of pull." The Tenderloin minister claims that MCC officials pleaded with him to help their cause, but their sexist nature forbade him to make the move. Thus he is content to remain in the Tenderloin district of San Francisco and concern himself with social action and minority liberation. The same non-smoker and non-drinker who freely peppers his speech with profanity ("I talk in the vocabulary of my people") is currently waging a war against television, which he considers to be true pornography.

If Broshears is gay Christianity's social activist, Nicholas Benton is unquestionably the true revolutionary of the movement. A brilliant young radical, he was formerly the leader of the Gay Seminarians at the Pacific School of Religion — the group from which Bill Johnson emerged. Benton was on his way to becoming the first homosexual to be ordained, also by the United Church of Christ, when he was betrayed by those who had been supporting his gay position. While traveling to the place where he was to be questioned by an ecclesiastical council, a confidant asked him to deny his homosexuality and accept ordination. This experience embittered Benton and led him to withdraw from organized religion, stating publicly, "I feel that I am joining rather than leaving the church of God." Since that time he has wandered far from the convictions of mainline gay Christianity and has, as a result, lost the support of most of the gays who had previously admired him. Striking out at the white, middle-class, male, capitalist mentality of MCC, Benton charged the fellowship with self-righteous and traitorous attitudes. Jim Sandmire's response was calm:

> He's brilliant, but he's done a great deal of damage . . . not because of his ideas particularly, but because of the way he has expressed them. Like a good many people who are very strong in their ideas, he has become a hardened elitist who refuses to see much good in anybody other than those who share his own ideas.

Benton's ideas are not as conventional as Sandmire's words imply. Considering all of humanity to be basically homosexual, he feels that each individual is channeled into a specific orientation at a certain age. Since we all are fundamentally identical, the Berkeley intellectual predicts that it is only natural to expect individuals to recede into homosexual activity. This is true emancipation. Benton states, "I think all men want me to tell them to go queer, they are just afraid to admit it." His movement, however, is entitled "Effeminism," which basically argues that males, gay and straight, should divest themselves of the bondage of masculinity. The organization distributes reams of its propaganda (such as the booklet *Sexism, Racism and White Faggots in Sodomist Amerika*), but its intricate, pseudo-scholarly content sails far above the heads of most of the gay male population. Thus Benton satisfies himself with the publication of material more obscene than Broshears' speech, while the rest of the gay Christian movement travels a separate path.

Within the gay religious world, perhaps the most fascinating collective of ministers are what San Francisco *Examiner* religion writer Lester Kinsolving has termed "paper priests." Operating out of the Eastern Orthodox faith, they participate in mutual consecration services that begin at priesthood and end (at present) with Archbishop status. The only key is to find an individual of a higher rank who will volunteer for one reason or another to manufacture a promotion. When this is accomplished, the priest submerges himself in impressive clerical regalia and celebrates complex high Catholic masses that amuse the few curious gays who choose to gather. Before long, antagonisms among the clique develop and the members separate, each with the hope of finding a new means of justifying his self-made religious world.

Father Gerard (also known as Father Lawrence and Father Smith) is one such example. At his St. Procupuis Rectory (Oblates of St. Jude) in San Francisco, there is a congregation estimated at one hundred, which is somewhat incredible considering the countless religious statues, icons, altars, mementos, and vestments that crowd the tiny apartment. Father Gerard's official stationery displays a Bishop's seal that he picked up from a local printer, "I don't know whose it is — probably some bishop who died" (the seal has since been tracked to the Bishop of San Diego). The young, mysterious gay priest claims to have been ordained by a "bishop of an Orthodox body" but is unable to produce any ordination papers. Commenting on his colleagues, he states very solemnly:

> I am my own. I don't associate with anyone. The rest of them are "play-church fanatics" who are on ego trips. They are jealous of me because I am doing a better job than they are. There are a lot of phonies around, and you'd better look out for them.

One of those whom Gerard was referring to was the Rt. Rev. Jonathon Schneider, who is the Prefect of the Missionaries of St. Augustine of the Syro-Chaldean Church and part-time MCC member. In a home that greatly resembles Father Gerard's chapel, Schneider sits in clerical robes behind a desk cluttered with religious articles and a semi-nude male doll. His dream is to found a small monastery in the country. The former theatrical fashion designer speaks of his church, his order, his priests, and his parishes, but for the homosexuals in his community, Schneider's ministry is lost somewhere in the files on his desk.

One of the paper priests who has come to the attention of the public is the Rev. Robert Richards. As a result of a series of articles by Kinsolving (whose columns are carried by over 230 papers across the nation), Richards was exposed as a homosexual with an FBI record, impersonating a Roman Catholic priest. His response was a two million dollar law suit against Kinsolving for the alleged libelous remarks.

The story of this gay priest has long been a mystery to the gay community he served and is related here as accurately as possible. Born Robert Tato, he left the Roman Catholic Church in his early twenties to become an Eastern Orthodox Catholic. He was training at the time to become a police officer in San Diego, but abandoned his work to follow a call into the ministry. These plans were temporarily delayed when he was imprisoned at Terminal Island for three months, the result of a draft resistance conviction. After his release in 1968 he was ordained to the priesthood of the Antiochian Orthodox Archdiocese of Toledo, Ohio, under

the name of Robert Tato. During a ministry in Gaines-
ville, Ohio, however, he was charged with the sexual
solicitation of a 15-year-old male. The priest never
appeared in court, choosing rather to jump bail and
change his name to Bob Richards. Followed by the
FBI, he entered a monastery in Utah, where a Catholic
priest persuaded him to reenter the Roman faith. He
was reinstated in 1969 by a former hospital chaplain,
after which he established the Community of St. John
the Beloved, "a Catholic worker commune serving the
Homophile community of San Francisco." At this point,
he emotionally claimed that he had been suspended from
the priesthood by the Archbishop, presumably for his
gay worship services. Archbishop McGucken of San
Francisco states, "I have never suspended him; he was
never given any faculties of the Roman Catholic priesthood which could be suspended." The announcement
left Richards in something of a dilemma: he was a
Roman Catholic church member and an Antiochian
Orthodox priest, but not a Roman Catholic priest nor
an Antiochian Orthodox church member. In the midst
of the confusion, Richards applied for funding as a gay
minister for the Quakers, which prompted his Antiochian
bishop to release him from the church (to which he no
longer belonged) because "his homosexuality has no
place in the pulpit." Not one to sit idly by, Bob Richards
quickly announced his acceptance into the American
Orthodox church, headed by the Rt. Rev. Robert M.
Clement of New York. Discussing Robert (Tato) Richards, a fellow gay priest summed the matter up succinctly: "He embarrasses everybody."

Should the tale of Richards seem absurd, it is at
least equaled by the story of Mikhail Itkin (born Itkin-
sky), known in the gay world as "the gay pope." Not one
leader in the gay community can discuss the bishop
without a chuckle. He is the epitome of religiosity,
having mastered every rite, ritual, and regulation in the
Greek, Antiochian, and Roman Catholic liturgies. He
also has the singular distinction of having memorized

every stage cue for the coronation of the pope. In an autobiography, the prelate succinctly states his position to be a

> Bishop with the Evangelical Catholic Community of the Love of Christ, a province of the Syro-Chaldean United Episcopal Church, and minister to the Radical Gay Christians at the Congregation of Jesus our Brother in Hollywood (Bishop Mikhail Itkin, *The Radical Jesus and Gay Consciousness*).

Included in his long list of educational credits is a "D.G.S." — Doctor of Gay Studies, from Quest Institute. Born in New York City in 1936, Itkin has become a byword in the homophile community. He briefly applied for membership in MCC, but, as one Fellowship Elder stated, "We didn't figure he had it together." He retaliated by charging the gay church with sexism and printed leaflets to that effect and distributed them in San Francisco. Ray Broshears, though no advocate of MCC, sent him to Los Angeles:

> Several of us took up the money to make sure he would go. We put him on the bus. My God! We said "Oh L.A., we love you. A plague on your house!"

Thus he arrived in Los Angeles, where John Hose, then the associate pastor of the Mother Church, counseled with him. Hose candidly judges the Bishop:

> I suspect that what he's doing is playing church. Mike's a sharp person, and I like him personally, but I've told him to his face that he's full of shit, to put it very bluntly. I don't think that most people are going to come and participate in a thing just because they need pomp and circumstance. They can go join the Masons if they want to put on funny uniforms and march down the street.

Jonathon Schneider, one of Itkin's priests, eagerly relates tales of his superior that are repeated from bar to bar. For instance, in Minnesota Itkin was asked to dedicate a chapel, but after arriving, reportedly held an orgy in the sanctuary instead. There is also the case of Nazarin Bashir Ahmed who, on the night before his ordination into the priesthood was scheduled, decided to become a Christian, prompting Schneider to remark, "He was one of Itkin's rush jobs. It was a very sloppy thing." The inner workings of the Itkin organization are equally intriguing.

> Itkin gets a small group of good men around him, ordains them, and then starts a fight with them. Then they are usually excommunicated. Just recently he lifted all excommunications. When he gets in a fight with someone, he publishes a new "rule book" which gives him more authority and that way he is unbeatable. The secret is to find the "rule book" that you came in on and argue under those rules.

Schneider is currently President of the United Syro-Chaldean Episcopal Synod, which is the body of Itkin's consecrated priests. It acts as an appeal board in the case of an excommunication. Already active, the Synod recently reversed an excommunication.

Despite the ridicule that plagues Itkin's life, he nevertheless has experienced oppression far more real than most gay Christians. In a two-month period in 1972, his chapel was desecrated three times by "Jesus Freaks." The first incident occurred on May 14 when four men burst in screaming, "You can't be queer and Christian!" and threatened violence if the radical gay Christians continued holding public worship services. Three weeks later, one of the men returned before the scheduled services shouting, "The Homo church is still operating and we warned you to stop!" Bishop Itkin, who had been showering, ran into the chapel clutching a towel, only to face the man flinging a 70-pound stone table at him. It missed its target but shattered the altar. Finally, on July 15, the group invaded the chapel a third time, stabbing a 15-year-old boy and spattering the apartment with human excrement. Mikhail Itkin would seem to offer the gay community two things it needs: a martyr and a comic.

This chapter, at best, can merely serve as an introduction to the intricate complexities which form gay religion. At this point each facet is a variable that may ultimately create a uniform body, but now stretches and tears at itself. If it were not for common conviction and zeal, the gay church would undoubtedly splinter and disintegrate. Will the United Church of Christ remain open to the gay question, or was Johnson's ordination a token move? Will the success of fundamentalist groups on gay churches continue to be tolerated? Can MCC afford to encourage Harrison's flirtation with the American Baptists? Will Dignity be crushed by Rome? Is it conceivable for Clement, Broshears, and Benton to join forces? Will MCC be their common ground? Will the role of the "paper priests" prove crucial or insignificant in the movement? These are questions for which only time has the answers. The few clues that have been provided will form the content of Chapter 9.

7: Don We Now Our Gay Apparel

Despite its denials — and its intentions — MCC is indeed a "gay church." We are told that it is "just like any other Christian church" and it is widely advertised as being a church for "all people." MCC pastors and leaders acknowledge that their ministry to date has been directed largely at the gay community and that only a small percentage of their membership is non-gay. However, they dislike being referred to as a gay church. One prominent MCC pastor told us:

> There are Christian churches, there are Jewish temples, and there are Buddhist temples . . . but there is no gay church. I don't subscribe to these half-assed theories that God is gay or anything like that. That is ridiculous as far as I'm concerned.

It is our contention that MCC and other gay religious groups are merely an extension of the gay life-style clothed in religiosity. This is *not* to say that church leaders and laymen are insincere in their desire to minister to the spiritual needs of the gay community. Even a superficial acquaintance with these groups leaves the impression that they are accomplishing much good, and no one can doubt that many gays have experienced profound spiritual change as a result of their association with MCC. Some even claim physical healing, as indicated by the following account (in *The Gay Christian*) describing what happened to a member of the Denver church as he approached the Communion rail during an Annual Conference worship service.

> For a number of years, he had been plagued by advancing deafness. He was forced to use a hearing aid. Suddenly there was a loud screeching noise in his ears. He thought that his hearing aid had shorted out. He removed it and started hearing strange noises — people whispering, feet sliding along the floor, papers rustling — sounds he had not heard in years. Incredulously he approached the Communion rail and partook of the elements. Then he ran out of the sanctuary and sat on the curb, weeping. The sounds were so loud, they were painful (October 1972).

Gay churches maintain that because of their ministry to the gay community they must retain certain linkages with the secular homosexual world just as straight churches must remain in touch with the larger secular world. Furthermore, they argue, their gay life-style is not inconsistent with their Christianity. Why, then, should they drop out of a way of life that is perfectly natural to them?

Their interpretation of the familiar "in the world but not of the world" notion is not really analogous to that preached by the straight evangelical churches with which they ostensibly identify. Neither is it correct that gay churches reflect no more of the homosexual subculture than non-gay churches mirror the heterosexual world, as some MCC people contend.

We believe that a case can be made for contending that the gay church is simply another arm of the gay world by even a casual analysis of the general life of the church, especially as evidenced in its official publications. No one can read MCC newsletters, magazines, and other published material and come away with the feeling that one has been exposed to publications that are "just like" those produced by other evangelical, Protestant denominations and local churches. Though the gay church seeks to promote the image of a "typical Christian church," the trappings of the gay world clearly show through their religious garb, at least to the outside observer.

For example, this bit of verse by "Desperate Desmond" published in *The Prodigal,* an "organ of Christian outreach" distributed by MCC-San Diego, only reinforces the commonly held notion that homosexuals are preoccupied with sex:

INSIDE JOB

I'm your gay exterminator;
   I make ants go bye-bye.
I'm also a terror with mice;
   But I'll be gentle with your fly.

One of the hallmarks of the gay subculture, as noted by Martin Hoffman and others, is the obsession with sex that seems especially to pervade the *male* homosexual community. "It seems to me that the most striking thing about gay life in general, which differentiates it from the straight world, is that its participants devote an inordinate amount of time to sexual matters" (Hoffman, p. 75).

While members of MCC and other gay groups vigorously assert that sex is only a part of their life-style, their publications are not convincing on this point. Direct and indirect references to sex, "cruising," and related activities abound in the publications of some of the leading MCC congregations. One columnist for *The Prodigal* was especially criticized for the propriety of some of his remarks. One of the milder examples of his writing included this:

> Ron B. told me he shaved off his beard because it made him look too butch. (That is a contradiction in terms. Can anyone be *too* rich or *too* butch? If Ron could bottle it, he'd be both.) It would appear that whenever Ron got a number home, he would turn over before Ron got a chance to (December 3, 1972).

Another item in the same periodical announced an upcoming social event — a "Good Ferry Lollipop" cruise aboard the *Marietta*. It was noted that "costumes" are in order (drag) and "there would be dancing on one deck — a show . . . a darkened upper deck, and two bars — one serving mixed drinks." The notice concludes with a not-so-subtle allusion: "Bids on the crew don't appear to be in order — yet" (February 20, 1972).

Gossip and humor columns in these publications seem to show an obsession with restroom jokes. The following comes from *The Catalyst* in Denver:

> I chiseled my name and phone number in every restroom, men's and women's, just in case, in town. I also hit every pay phone and a good number of Yellow Cabs too. You should see my nails, they're just shot. And the worst part of all, my number's been changed" (April 9-23, 1972).

An advertisement for a bookkeeping service proclaims: "Don't get screwed by IRS . . . . . . let us do it — your Income Tax" (*The Prodigal,* February 20, 1972).

In all fairness it should be said that some members of MCC are quite concerned about this kind of writing and do not condone the use of suggestive material in church publications. The editorial policy of *The Channel,* published by MCC-Dallas, states that only "material of a discreet high caliber" will be sought and that the editors "intend to provide material beneficial to the spiritual growth of our readers" (January 7, 1973). The point remains, however, that it would be difficult to find counterparts in heterosexual or straight churches for some of the material widely distributed in MCC circles.

We have already commented on the prominence of gay bars in the homosexual subculture and MCC's outreach to the gay bar scene. Hoffman writes:

> The gay bar plays a central role in the life of very many homosexuals — one which is much more important than the role played by straight bars in the life of all but a few heterosexuals. This is connected intimately with the use of the gay bar as a sexual marketplace and, of course, with the fact that homosexuals have really no place where they can congregate without disclosing to the straight world that they are homosexual (p. 51).

Although the gay church "officially" views the bar primarily as a location for evangelism (as noted in Chapter 4), their use for ·other purposes is clearly not frowned on. And, unlike many conservative evangelicals, gay Christians do not proscribe social drinking. The following quote does little to disguise the obvious enthusiasm with which the Denver Couples' Club pursues its soul-winning in gay bars:

> Our Saturday night roller skating party turned out to be an evening at Shakey's Pizza Parlor, for pizza and beer. Then we were off to the bars for bar evangelism and distributing of posters for Troy Perry's meetings. All had a "Gay" ol' time (*The Catalyst,* April 9-23, 1972).

Another issue of the same church newsletter states: "One of the most interesting experiences that I think anyone could have is to go to Our Den [a Denver bar] after Sunday night service to see what is happening!!!!!!!!" (June 18-July 2, 1972). However, another issue of *The Catalyst* offers this warning to bar fanciers:

> Several of our compatriots have learned the hard way that it just isn't safe to leave the bars with strangers, no matter how goodlooking or innocent they appear nor what a good time they promise. Unfortunately there are still many straights who find us gays easy marks. Play it safe and don't pick a trick until you've seen him around enough and observed enough to be sure his friends are not waiting for you behind a tree or that he will not hold a knife to your throat in his car (July 17-July 30, 1972).

The *New Life Outreach,* published by MCC-Philadelphia, describes one western-leather bar in the city of brotherly love as being "the unofficial watering-hole for some of the MCC members during the week and weekends" (February/March, 1972). The same newsletter suggests that the reader check out a new bar featuring dancing and "a lot of young(er) chicks." Full-page ads for public establishments frequented by gays are not uncommon in MCC publications. One bar is described on a two-page spread as "the bar that cares about you." The very next page of the newsletter contains a poem about the Friend of the friendless — Jesus Christ. "Through all your cares and sorrow He is waiting for you, with a love that is true." Another ad in the magazine of MCC-San Francisco is for a club featuring nude go-go boys.

The gay bars are illustrative of the fast-paced social life typical of much of the gay world. "Primarily a social milieu, the gay world opens up a whole new range of potential acquaintances and opportunities for entertainment. If one is reasonably attractive and outgoing, one can rapidly develop a busy social life" (Fisher, p. 240). This facet of gay life also is reflected in the gay church. A look at a typical church social calendar will reveal a round of activities unequaled in most straight churches (though this is perhaps more open to debate than other points made here, and gay Christians may indeed be correct in maintaining that they are no more involved in social activities than their non-gay counterparts). There are hay rides, beach parties, potluck dinners, picnics, hamburger fries, and rap sessions. The emphasis on "good times" is certainly familiar to anyone who has participated in high school and college youth group activities in straight churches.

Martin Hoffman writes that "being homosexual means belonging to an underground community of fellows which provides one with not only a sense of one's identity, but also with places to go and things to do . . ." (p. 150). MCC represents an extension of this "community of fellows" where good times are to be had with other gay Christians. The Denver church's newsletter proclaims:

> So many new places to go; so many new things going on at the old spots. . . . Good times were also abundant at MCC's second annual free Christmas Party on Dec. 22nd. Good times, good friends, good snacks, and dancing all were available (*The Catalyst,* December 1972-January 14, 1973).

MCC-San Diego announced that the "kickoff" for its annual Spiritual Renewal would begin with the New

Year's Eve service, to be followed by a "Watch Party" to be "held in the social hall, with dancing, entertainment, and a gala welcome to 1973" (*The Prodigal,* December 17, 1972). Just a few weeks earlier, the same newsletter announced a "Gala Christmas Carnival" affording the opportunity to "Kiss the cuties and hit the pastors with wet sponges!"

"Since virtually the sole criterion of value in the homosexual world is physical attractiveness, being young and handsome in gay life is like being a millionaire in a community where wealth is the only criterion of value" (Hoffman, p. 153). This characteristic of the gay sub-culture also is manifested in the literature published by gay churches.

> The gossip brigade at H & S had a field day one recent evening when a certain well-known older-but-nice character came in with an extremely handsome young newcomer. The gossip soared to new levels when the young chap who has been seen with the OBN character then arrived with a love of his own — and they made a very friendly foursome (*Catalyst,* July 17-July 30, 1972).

In a column appropriately entitled, "Cruise News," in *The MCC Crusader,* published by the Tampa church, the same theme comes through: "David E., we missed you and your new boyfriend Kack at Church, and we are wondering, Honey, iffin' you're 'fraid to bring him with you so that others can see how handsome he is???" (December, 1972). Later in the same column even the pastor does not escape comment:

> Our Handsome Pastor, it seems, doesn't have a big enough field to pick from so he is trying the University of Tampa with the excuse that he is going to be on the Staff as Advisor to the Students and Teachers. You can be sure there is a method in his madness. He won't be single long if he has all that to look over.

An ad for a bar asks the question, "Looking for the People?" and then goes on to promise "always BEAUTIFUL NEW PEOPLE." The constant search for new experience is illustrated in still another "opinion" column in *The Prodigal.* Describing his recent trip to Hawaii, the writer states:

> Now the trip that I went on was really not a pleasure trip; but I don't miss any opportunities. I checked out the parks and the T-rooms thoroughly. . . . I suppose that Waikiki in Honolulu has got to be one of the best cruising areas in the world. . . . Then of course the climate is so warm that the streets are full of shirtless, short-panted, male beauty (December 17, 1972).

The only real difference between the gay world of the homosexual church and the secular gay world is that the former includes a religious or spiritual dimension that often appears (to the non-gay observer at best) to be tacked on in an attempt at securing moral legitimacy for homosexual behavior. As we have tried to show, the combining of the spiritual with the social and sexual components of gay life often results in contradictions that the gay church would be hard pressed to explain. The gay parishioner will earnestly and sincerely describe some recent spiritual experience and virtually in the same breath passionately describe his latest conquest or the "good times" the boys had on the town the other night.

It is not difficult to lead a very lonely and unhappy life in the gay world. Beyond the surface glamour and excitement of the social whirl there is often disappointment, disillusionment, and isolation. Churchill writes of "the fruitless search for permanent love" and the "make-believe atmosphere" which permeates gay social relationships — "the pretentious claims to glamour, the petty rivalries, the frequent bouts of jealousy, envy, and remorse" (p. 193). He concludes that "In reality it is quite obvious that there is very little that is very gay about homosexuality or those who are homosexual in our society" (p. 191).

A recent article in the *Advocate* laments the fact that despite continuing efforts in the gay movement to improve the situation, loneliness and isolation remain the primary disabilities of the gay world. Study groups and rap sessions are not the answer:

The larger, ostensibly "social" homophile get-togethers all invariably resemble gay bars: the charged atmosphere of tension and sexual nervousness; the impossibility of even the simplest form of conversation; the defensive withdrawals into protective shells . . . (July 4, 1973, p. 37).

The gay church is aware of this problem and offers Christ and Christian love as the solution to perennial loneliness. In an article entitled, "The Gay Life is Rough," a gay Christian discusses the dilemma and its resolution:

How can so many lonely people do so much interacting with each other and still be so lonely? Is it because they're basically selfish, and make no real effort to build real friendships? This is often the case, but there is still something missing. Love. . . . Love is not just being able to hit it off with your latest trick for a couple weeks. . . . Love is also being able to enjoy drag queens, leather queens, dirty old men and dizzy chickens, as well as straights.

With a little love spread all around you, the gay life — or any other life—can be tremendous. At MCC we call it Christian spirit (*The Catalyst,* January 16-23, 1972).

In an effort to "talk out" some of the problems which confront gay people, most MCC churches sponsor weekly Rap Sessions dealing with such topics as: "Living with Heterosexuals," "Harassment," "The Leather Scene," and "Prejudice Within the Gay Community." An article entitled "What to Do When Arrested" appeared in an MCC publication as well as one called "Our Gay Legacy."

MCC publications are designed to reach the unchurched in the gay community. Nothing communicates this better than the "Statement of Policy" which appears in each issue of MCC *Cross Currents,* published by the San Francisco church. The statement indicates that many of the articles will deal with MCC personalities, activities, and church business.

We recognize, however, a responsibility to the gay community at large, and it is our intent to publish articles which will be of interest outside of our own mission and, we sincerely hope, outside of the church altogether. Only through the use of material which is provocative, yet tasteful, can we hope to reach out to our brothers and sisters who do not yet know of us, attract them to us, and thus fulfill the second basic purpose of this magazine (Spring 1973).

The same magazine, which bills itself as a "religious publication," adorned the cover of its premier issue with a photograph of two nude men sharing a cup of communion wine in front of a rustic, wood cross. Whether the photo was "provocative, yet tasteful," others will have to judge; one thing is certain, though: it was surely unusual vis-à-vis the average religious magazine. The first issue also contains a centerfold depicting a nude male playing a flute in the forest with a calendar of social events superimposed on the sylvan scene.

To list more of the numerous examples of incongruity in gay church publications would only reinforce what we have already noted: the gay church will have a difficult time convincing straight churches that they are not an extension of the gay world and that they are really serious about their spiritual mission. At the September 1972 General Conference of the Universal Fellowship of Metropolitan Community Churches, a leading spokesman for the gay denomination publicly indicated that "MCC recognizes its primary function to be an instrument of God to be used in bringing the wider Christian community into a renewed awareness and appreciation of the Gospel of Jesus Christ" (*The Gay Christian,* October 1972). If MCC expects to engage in meaningful dialogue with the "wider Christian community," especially the conservative evangelical segment of that community, it will first have to shed its gay apparel before getting down to the basic questions of theology and biblical interpretation that now separate the gay church from the traditional churches. To expect otherwise would be to hope for sociological miracles.

As it now stands, the straight Christian still associates the member of a gay church with a deviant, cultic aggregate. And, as we have indicated, the public relations efforts of the gay church have themselves fostered this image. At the same time it cannot be denied that for

the individual gay Christian, the gay church is indeed
functional. What Martin Hoffman says regarding the gay
community in general clearly applies to the gay church
as well: ". . . it makes him a member of a deviant community, and wherever he goes he can find a small group
of individuals who will have something in common with
him which is very real and very intrinsic to their own
being" (p. 150). In short, the gay church, like the gay
world, provides both a sense of identity and a community of fellows. Should spiritual benefits also accrue to
the individual, so much the better.

*The Homosexual Church
and Gay Liberation*

8: Gay, Proud, and Christian

Homosexuals constitute perhaps the largest minority group in America, and they are no longer a silent minority. The gay community is experiencing a growing militancy, particularly among younger, so-called "radical" homosexuals. Like other minority groups, the homosexual minority is organizing, and "like the champions of civil rights, peace, ecological concern and women's liberation, the proponents of the 'lavender revolution' have laid their cause at the door of the church" ("The Church and Gay Liberation," Elliott Wright, *The Christian Century,* March 3, 1971, p. 281).

In a chapter in the book *The Other Minorities,* Franklin Kameny makes a convincing case for applying the term "sociological minority" to the homosexual. Gay people are subject to prejudice and discrimination because of their sexual orientation and are subjected to the "profound depersonalization and deindividualization" of derogatory stereotypes (pp. 52-53). In response to society's attitudes toward him, the homosexual experiences alienation from the larger society and often expresses hostility toward it. A sense of "we" and "they" develops within the gay subculture and, Kameny states, "the community is formally organized, both in terms of inner directed group interests, and in terms of action directed toward altering the attitudes and actions of the majority which create the minority state" (p. 55).

Gay activists are working to end discrimination and prejudice against homosexuals by seeking to change the attitudes of the majority, eliminating stereotypes, and by promoting legislative change of sex laws. But they are also attempting to "raise the consciousness levels" of homosexuals themselves by countering the lowered self-image and lack of self-esteem that is often a by-product of society's negative attitudes. As Kameny puts it,

> A systematic effort is being made to instill into the homosexual a sense of his own worth; of pride in his homosexuality; of confidence in homosexuality as a way of life as rewarding and satisfying to the homosexual as heterosexuality is to the hetero-sexual, and not only harmless to society but one in which the homosexual can potentially live a life useful and productive to society if society will allow him to do so; of the full equality of homosexuality with heterosexuality; of his moral right to be homosexual and to live his homosexuality, fully, freely, openly, and with dignity, free of arrogant and insolent pressures upon him to convert to the prevailing heterosexuality (p. 62).

The emergence of the gay liberation movement is usually traced to the Christopher Street or Stonewall Riot in New York City's Greenwich Village. This erupted when the police raided the Stonewall Inn, a gay bar on Christopher Street. Such raids were not in themselves unusual, but this time the normally docile gays did not remain passive. They became angered and fought back, and the police had to barricade themselves inside the bar until reinforcements arrived. Word of the confrontation spread throughout the gay community and during the next few days gay people continued to battle police with shouts of "Gay Power!"

For the first time, large numbers of gay people came "out of the closet and into the street," a phrase frequently used to describe this new kind of homosexual militancy. Out of this gay protest the Gay Liberation

Front was formed, and later similar activist organizations were organized in the fight for homosexual freedom across the nation.

Each year on the anniversary of the Christopher Street uprising homosexuals in several large cities commemorate the event by staging parades and other festivities in order to demonstrate their continuing support for equal rights and "gay pride." Several thousand people participated in New York's first Christopher Street Parade on Gay Liberation Day in 1970. The same year a "Christopher Street West" celebration was organized in Hollywood, and in subsequent years the gay marches spread to other cities. In June 1973 more than two thousand gay people participated in the San Francisco Gay Freedom Day Parade, which featured colorful floats, lavender banners, balloons announcing "Gay is Good," and chants of "2-4-6-8, Gay is Just as Good as Straight!"

In an informative book on the homosexual liberation movement, sociologist Laud Humphreys explains the nature of the oppression gay people experience:

> Job discrimination, criminalization, a host of more subtle social assaults have produced alienation and self-hatred among homosexuals. They have been victimized by gangs of youths, the police, syndicated crime, physicians and social scientists, the military, their own families, and even those who share their own sexual preferences. Even in prison, they are segregated and, frequently, subject to rape. Perhaps most intolerable is the incessant need to pass, to hide their identities, aspirations, attitudes, and needs behind a facade of normalcy (*Out of the Closets*, p. 9).

Under the banner, "Gay is Good," Gay Lib has achieved the status of a major social movement in an extremely short time. Since the official birth of gay liberation in mid-1969, the homophile movement (which had been around for years in the relatively quiet form of organizations like the Mattachine Society and ONE, Inc.) experienced what Humphreys terms "an amazing surge of vitality" (p. 6). However, it soon became apparent

that a generation gap existed in the homophile movement
and a rift developed between the "older champions of
the homosexual cause" and the more youthful "new
radicals" or "gayrevs" (Humphreys, pp. 115-119).

> Some gay liberationists have become concerned about this
> problem of liberating the older homosexuals as well as the
> young. The Homophile Union of Boston has tried a special
> program, Gay Maturity Caucus, for gays over 35, while other
> organizations have been accused of being little more than
> "Associations of Senior Citizens." The new gay churches . . .
> may provide answers for aging homosexuals who feel unwanted
> (Humphreys, p. 119).

Social analysts trace the roots of the gay liberation
movement to the civil rights and student protest movements of the 1960s. Like the Jesus movement, gay liberation is also said to have been spawned by the feelings
of disaffiliation and disenchantment characterizing the
counter culture. Humphreys, for example, sees the street
people as setting the stage for the gay revolution. "It
[the counter culture] supplied special skills, an ideology,
and the necessary reinforcement to increase autonomy for
the youthful gays" (p. 113).

Whatever its sources, the gay liberation movement
has had tremendous impact upon the entire homosexual
scene. It has meant a revolution of life-style, just as
women's liberation has questioned the old ways and
restrictive norms of a male-dominated society. It has
even brought new meaning to the word "gay" as Peter
Fisher notes in *The Gay Mystique:*

> Today, more and more homosexuals identify themselves as gay
> — with pride, sometimes with anger. The word has become
> an assertion of identity and legitimacy. It is a word of con-
> frontation: it says, I define myself — you do not define me.
> "Gay" is to "homosexual" as "black" is to "Negro" (p. 233).

Every liberation movement has its moral or religious
dimension and gay liberation is no exception. Humphreys
observes that there is a tendency for this moral force to
become institutionalized in organized religion and he
labels the Metropolitan Community Church as "an early,

thoroughly institutionalized product of gay liberation"
(p. 11).

Troy Perry envisioned his church's role in the struggle
for the homosexual's civil rights from the very beginning.

> We had to take a militant, nonviolent stand against the kind of
> dehumanizing brutality and harassment we were up against.
> But those of us who had been through it knew that we would
> never be pushed again without standing up for our rights. We
> would never stand in the shadows. We would never hide our
> faces again. We would stand in the sunshine. We would stand
> with our heads held high, never again bowed low. We would
> know that God was with us, and that we were His children.
> We were on His side. We would never again be afraid of what
> society could do to us (Perry, p. 154).

Perry describes a parade in which his congregation
participated:

> We were the last in this smoothly run parade. I rode in an
> open convertible. Behind me came the congregation singing
> "Onward Christian Soldiers." We were gay, and we were
> proud. We had come out of our closets and into the streets.
> We were applauded — I think it was for our courage, and a
> kind of recognition for what we were doing in the religious
> community. It was a moving experience (p. 167).

Some time later Rev. Perry led a prayer vigil and fast
on Hollywood Boulevard in order to bring attention to
the need for revision of what he termed "unjust" sex
laws. He was arrested for blocking the sidewalk.

Gay churches have always supported gay liberation
organizations and activities. While perhaps not aligning
themselves with the more radical elements in the movement, they have consistently participated in activist causes,
supported Gay Pride Day, and marched in gay-sponsored
parades. In San Francisco's Gay Freedom Day Parade
(June 1973), MCC was represented by a large group of
members singing hymns and "We Shall Overcome."
MCC-Philadelphia publishes a newsletter with announcements of homophile activities in the greater Philadelphia
area. The February-March 1972 issue, for example, lists
classes on gay sexuality at a local "Free University,"
mentions a coffee hour sponsored by "Students for Indi-

vidual Rights," announces the up-coming programs of the local Gay Activists Alliance (GAA), notes that the Homophile Action League (HAL) meets the first and third Wednesday of each month and sponsors a monthly gay dance, and, finally, invites readers to attend the coffee hour of the Gay Liberation Front at Temple University.

The Circle of Friends, billed as "the oldest homophile organization in Texas," holds its regular meetings twice monthly in the facilities of MCC-Dallas. The COF is described as an "educational/political organization that seeks to create a better understanding of the gay life-style and greater political support of needed changes to laws affecting the gay person" (*The Channel*, January 7, 1973). In San Francisco, the tax-exempt Council on Religion and the Homosexual sponsored a benefit auction on Mother's Day for the Lesbian Mothers Union. The local MCC was also represented at the event. And in Seattle, a coalition of gay organizations formed to combat increased police entrapment and harassment included the Metropolitan Community Church in its membership.

The sermon for the chartering service of MCC-Philadelphia was entitled "Our Emancipation Proclamation." Reading it exposes one to the liberationist rhetoric characteristic of the movement for homosexual freedom:

> We recognize our supreme indebtedness to the so-called minorities of the world: by whatever names we are called, who have, and are, by their good deeds, showing the sacredness of human worth that is rightfully ours; the *right to be ourselves as God made us.*
>
> With all of our desires to raise the consciousness of society to the rights and needs of all minorities and total society, let us not forget in our efforts that God, by whatever Name you know and love, is above all and is already making ways for us to have our deliverances from oppressions (*New Life Outreach*, September/October, 1972).

This same theme is found in an article entitled "Christian

Liberation" in MCC's denominational magazine *In Unity:*

> The primary reason for Christ's sacrifice was not merely to
> liberate us from the hold of oppressive sin, but to free us so
> we could develop lifestyles based on brotherly love and self-
> respect. . . . A Homosexual Christian lifestyle is what we
> should be liberated for! And when we have achieved this state
> of living, liberation from all of the social oppression that
> homosexuals suffer will inevitably follow because IF GOD
> IS FOR US, WHO CAN BE AGAINST US? (April 1971,
> p. 9).

The notion that "God is on our side" is certainly not
uncommon when one looks at the many social and
religious movements of our day. This form of "legitimacy
by association" is very prevalent in the literature and
public pronouncements of the gay church. As we pointed
out in Chapter 3, some gay churchmen have asserted that
God has elected to make the gay condition his condition,
and that he is not neutral in the matter. Howard Wells
describes God as "a God of liberation, who calls to himself the oppressed and abused and assures them that his
righteousness will vindicate their suffering" (*The Gay
Christian,* September 1972). The ancient Israelites
exemplify the oppressed minority with God on its side:

> As the enslaved Jewish people in Egypt called him the God
> of Israel, and today, as black people who are discovering
> their identity and oneness with God, are referring to him as
> their "black God," we, the gay community, have the right to
> refer to our liberator, our redeemer, as our "gay God."

The vulnerable point in the comparison of gay with
black liberation is that blacks are undeniably born with
their skin color, whereas it is not generally agreed that
homosexuals are born gay. As we have stressed elsewhere, however, most gay Christians do subscribe to
the view that they were born homosexual and often
speak in terms of "my God-given homosexual identity."
The black-gay analogy is delineated by MCC's
Howard Wells, who claims that "straight" Christian
theology should be rejected for its failure to recognize

the plight of gay people, just as it neglects the needs of oppressed blacks.

> Such a straight theology only presents to the gay person the unacceptable option of being the "good queer," the homosexual who stays in his place, meek and mild, a gay Uncle Tom, the "homo" who avoids any public reference to his sexual orientation in the company of nice, polite straight people, the gay who is the analogy of the Negro trying to be white. Instead of hiding it, to be human in a condition of social oppression always involves affirming that which the oppressor regards as de-grading, not pretending that it does not exist or trying to hide it! For gay people, that means affirming our sexuality loud and clear! Such affirmation will be our salvation (*The Gay Christian*, September 1972).

To follow such advice, at least for Christians who are gay, would mean that participation in demonstrations and marches would have particular merit and perhaps fulfil the biblical injunction to work out one's own salvation. Indeed, this sentiment was exemplified by the Rev. Robert Clement of the Church of the Beloved Disciple of New York. Along with the Rev. Paul Breton of MCC-Washington, Clement participated in a march to the Connecticut State Capitol in October 1971 in celebration of that state's new sex law making homosexual acts legal between consenting adults. In his gold and scarlet robes, Clement proclaimed: "The greatest sin you can commit is to deny being gay. If you accept yourself, you're accepting God in His perfection" (*Advocate*, October 1971). Referring to the role of gay churches, Clement observed on the same occasion: "We exist to upset, bother, and annoy the consciences of all the straight churches."

Troy Perry once marched to a State Capitol also. In June of 1971 he and a group of followers marched from San Francisco to Sacramento to dramatize what they felt were needed reforms in California sex laws. At the State Capitol Building, they were addressed by Assemblyman Willie Brown, who offered support and encouragement for their efforts. Perry describes the memorable event:

> Then, a very strange thing happened. A halo appeared around the sun just as we asked for a sign from God that we were

doing the right thing. Reverend Howard Wells summed it up
when he said, "God has shown He is with us, and if God be
with us, who can be against us" (p. 211).

As in other protest movements, there are those gays who
believe that violent confrontations with the Establishment
are inevitable. Over against that sentiment, the Metropolitan Community Churches and other gay religious
groups have been a voice of moderation. Writing on
"Violence and the Gay Christian," Howard Wells states
that it is imperative for gay Christians to evaluate the
nature of their response in the event that confrontations
do become violent. Wells points to Christ's Sermon on
the Mount for guidance and concludes that one must
always be careful to avoid returning violence with violence.

> The gay Christian does not run away from violent confronta-
> tions with oppression when there are no alternatives to elimi-
> nating it. Rather, the gay Christian *embraces* the violence
> directed at him, smothering it with love, and endures the per-
> sonal suffering that is commensurate with such action. In effect,
> the voluntary suffering of the oppressed for the sake of waking
> up the oppressor to his sins is the final, redeeming agent of
> reconciliation. When everything else fails, suffering for the
> sake of love works (*New Life Outreach*, July/August 1972).

The gay Christians are militant in proclaiming that
what they want is neither sympathy nor token toleration,
but total acceptance. They are unequivocally gay, defi-
antly proud, and unashamedly Christian. They constitute
what Fisher terms the "new" homosexuals.

> The new homosexual today knows that there are other gay
> people and where they are to be found; he or she reads about
> them in the paper, sees them on TV, notices them on the street.
> Young gays may still have difficulty in accepting themselves at
> first, and they may be discouraged by public hostility toward
> homosexuals, but a new message reaches them which has never
> been voiced before: *Gay is good, gay is proud* (p. 232).

Nothing summarizes better the nature of the liberation message preached by the gay church than the
following statement appearing in an MCC publication:

If the MCC movement has anything to say to gay people, it is that the Gospel of Jesus Christ can liberate us from the need for *any* kind of closet. You are a child of God. If you begin to believe that, you will find yourself peeling off your closets, shedding them. God made you. He loves you. You have dignity (*The Gay Christian*, October 1972).

9: Keeping a Straight Face

In his book referred to earlier in this volume, Dr. Ronald L. Akers makes a statement about the rewards provided the homosexual through his participation in the gay subculture that applies equally to the gay church:

> In addition to a better organized set of justifications for his homosexuality, the homosexual community provides him with a ready sexual marketplace, social reinforcement, and group support for a deviant sexual activity. The gay world provides him with a supportive refuge in the realization that he is not alone. He can find a congenial atmosphere of acceptance where he can relax his "straight" front and become part of a network of friends with similar inclinations (pp. 162-163).

As one gay church member put it, "To many of us MCC has become a faith, a vocation, a social organization and a very important part of our everyday life." The gay church may indeed provide a spiritual refuge for its members, but as we have already noted, it also serves the wider function of legitimizing an entire life-style and easing the burden of social censure to which homosexuals are subjected. And there are some other advantages that accrue to members of gay religious organizations:

Due to the nation's tradition of religious freedom, gay churches enjoy some protection from legal and social stigma. This form of stigma redemption enables gays to deduct contributions to their cause from income taxes, as well as to profit from the tax-exempt status of their parsonages and meeting places. They can sponsor dances with little likelihood of police interference and provide an umbrella for a wide range of social, publishing, and service activities (Humphreys, p. 152).

The gay church is eager for acceptance in the religious and secular world alike. Gay churchmen point with pride to the measure of attention they have already received from liberal segments of the Christian community, such as the call for "full and complete acceptance" in a *Christian Century* editorial of March 3, 1971. The Metropolitan Community Churches have announced plans to apply for membership in the National Council of Churches, perhaps as early as the fall of 1974.

Gay religious leaders like Troy Perry have achieved some attention from politicians and civic leaders, who recognize the potential political force represented by the gay community. Not all gay ministers have the political connections that Perry does, however, and Perry himself no doubt overestimates his influence in the political arena. The public relations effort characteristic of the gay church is not unlike the larger homosexual minority which "mocks while at the same time imitating slavishly the standards of the majority, and would consider itself honored in the extreme if it could receive accolades from the Daughters of the American Revolution or the Knights of Columbus" (Churchill, p. 187). The MCC gives prominent display to the routine official congratulatory messages sent to member congregations by high-ranking public officials on special occasions such as the chartering of a new church. For example, when the Metropolitan Community Church of Philadelphia received its official charter, the church newsletter carried several full-page reproductions of congratulatory statements, including one issued by the Governor of Pennsylvania and one on the prestigious letterhead of the White

House and signed by a Special Assistant to the President. Appropriately, a newspaper account of the latter greeting appeared under the headline: "But Did the President Know?"

While the gay church seeks the plaudits of the straight world, its rank-and-file members are keenly aware that the time is far off when the non-gay majority will rise up and call them blessed. They often perceive themselves to be quite alone in their struggle for recognition. Tom Driver, writing in *Commonweal,* has rightly observed that "If a person's sexual identity is denied social sanction, he will appeal elsewhere — to nature, God, or the Devil" (April 6, 1973, p. 104). This, in a nutshell, is the story of the gay church. By appealing to God for His approval of their behavior, homosexuals are engaging in what Humphreys terms *stigma redemption.*

> More common is the attitude: "We may stand condemned in the courts of man but not before the throne of God!" Stigmatized persons redeem their own discredit by demanding reparation for suffering endured. They confront condemnation with their own moral indignation, cashing in a lifetime of stigma borne for the right to make moral demands on their accusers. This may be seen as a particularly effective method of countering oppression when employed by homosexuals and others whose reprobation is so often couched in the language of, and justified by, morality and religion (p. 149).

The concept of God's acceptance in the face of man's rejection is illustrated in an article written by Keith Delano Davis and published in the newsletter of MCC-Philadelphia.

> So, dearly beloved, we know that even as Jesus was falsely accused, we also will be falsely accused of ALL MANNER OF THINGS that "offends" the established authority, be it the traditional church, state or civil society. There are many who DO NOT WANT to see a church, such as the Metropolitan Community Church, succeed . . . for IT WILL SHOW THE LEADERS how much they, and society, have failed in meeting the needs of ALL of God's children. Society's REJECTION is God's ELECTION (*New Life Outreach,* February/March, 1972).

The success which MCC has enjoyed in the brief period since 1968 when it began in Troy Perry's living room is obvious when one looks at membership and other statistics. An article in a recent issue of the *Advocate* referred to the gay denomination as "the Western World's most effective force for gay liberation" (April 11, 1973). Obviously enthusiastic about the impact MCC is having in the homosexual world, a member writes in *MCC News:*

> Why then does MCC become bigger and a lot better each year with more and more members? Let me tell you why! Because we have Christ as our leader. . . . it is our accepting Him as our leader that has shown us the grand success we now enjoy. . . . It's obvious that Someone up there likes us and is willing to lend a hand when needed (June 18, 1972).

Can the "grand success" be expected to continue indefinitely? What future directions will the career path of MCC take? Although MCC-Seattle pastor Robert Sirico boasts, "We are the fastest growing church in Seattle," that is certainly not true of MCC congregations everywhere. A December 1972 issue of *The Prodigal* editorially complains about the attendance problem in San Diego and asks what can be done about it. The same article acknowledges, "The only conclusion that can be drawn is that MCC is somehow making the same errors that all of the established churches are making."

Perhaps the most serious indication that MCC is indeed going the way of other denominations came in the spring of 1973 when the flourishing Denver church announced that it had withdrawn from the MCC fellowship. Insiders felt that trouble had been brewing for some time and that a break was inevitable. In an official letter circulated publicly by the Denver congregation, the Board of Directors stated that the decision to withdraw was based on "an evident lack of concern on the part of the Board of Elders [of the denomination] for the spiritual growth of the member congregations of the fellowship, on apparently irreconcilable differences in denominational policies, and arbitrary nature of administrative decisions."

Battle lines were soon drawn on both sides of this explosive issue. Both sides claimed that the other misunderstood them. The split was a featured story in the *Advocate* and it appeared that, for the first time, Troy Perry's unquestioned leadership was being openly questioned. Although the details behind the Denver departure may never be ascertained, it is known that members of the Denver church were increasingly distressed by the political activism associated with the "Mother Church." Special displeasure was voiced concerning an invitation to California Assemblyman Willie Brown to address a 1972 conference of the gay denomination in San Francisco. It was felt that the presence of such "a partisan political figure" at a church meeting was inappropriate (*Advocate,* April 11, 1973).

Whether this event will trigger additional dissension within the ranks of MCC remains to be seen. The alleged centralization of most of the denomination's decision-making in the Los Angeles church plus the increasing diversity of the far-flung member congregations would seem to indicate that the role of trouble-shooter for the fellowship may indeed be more crucial for Troy Perry than his position as founder.

There are also signs that some member churches are finding their tolerance for the denomination's conservative image waning. One East Coast MCC pastor expressed his irritation with fundamentalists who were "so Goddamn hell-bent on saving souls" and who promoted "this Jesus-saves, trust-in-the-Lord crap." An editorial in the magazine of New York City's MCC states:

> MCC's reputation as a "fundamentalist Pentecostal" organization seems to us to be something less than the whole truth. While MCC *is* strong in the South and West, it is growing in other areas too. And even in the Bible belt, we have found its members more open-minded than intellectuals often give them credit for being (*The Gay Christian*, February 1973).

The same periodical mentions "frustrated gay religious liberals" who might consider establishing "a new liberal gay church" in competition with the more conservative MCC.

Regional differences, liberal-conservative divisions, and the diversity brought about by the prior church backgrounds (or lack thereof) of ministers and members — these all portend the possibility of future discord in MCC. Also, because the leadership and membership of MCC churches is so predominantly male, the charge of sexism is one which surely will receive increasing discussion. A larger issue that promises continuing debate is the question of whether religious gay people will continue in their separatist gay churches or whether they will seek to worship, with the acceptance they demand, in the mainline straight denominations.

It is our opinion that churches like MCC will persist and probably grow until each major city in the United States has at least one gay church. It is doubtful that they will ever become very large congregations (MCC-LA already appears to be leveling off in attendance and is clearly an exception in terms of size). It is even more doubtful that they will develop working relationships with many non-gay churches in the near future. It will be difficult for MCC or any other gay religious group to reorient the churchgoing public's attitude toward gay people. What Edward Sagarin said about the homosexual movement in general probably also applies to the gay church: "The contradictions in the homophile movement are likely to prevent it from becoming other than isolated and cultist, sinking deeper into untenable ideological distortion as it proclaims only that which its members want to hear and which they need (or feel they need) to believe" (p. 110). Paraphrasing Sagarin, its theology has led the gay church into a *cul-de-sac* where, despite itself, it has become associated with the encircling gay world and therefore separated from the non-gay man-in-the-pew.

MCC's Howard Wells admits that "experience seems

to indicate that at the present stage of dialogue most straights can only relate to gays on a paternal, person-to-person basis." But he strikes at the very heart of the issue when he continues: "Reconciliation between straight and gay Christians cannot develop until the former recognize that a homosexual orientation is a valid, God-given form of human sexuality" (*The Gay Christian,* February 1973).

Christians who are theologically conservative simply cannot affirm homosexuality as a valid behavior and life-style. Thus, the reconciliation of which Wells speaks is impossible without a major concession on either side of the theological fence. Christians who value orthodoxy and who are rationally committed to the Bible as the infallible Word of God, the only rule of faith and practice, cannot be expected to dismiss lightly what Klaus Bockmühl has called the "fantastic exegetic somersaults" gay churchmen have perpetrated in order to support their position (*Christianity Today,* February 16, 1973, p. 17). The gay church has developed a theological stance that becomes a mechanism for reconciling and justifying obviously contradictory views. The result, according to Dr. Carl Henry, is that "biblical condemnations of homosexuality become a jungle of nonsense" (*Is Gay Good?* p. 109).

Henry, a leading conservative evangelical theologian, contends that the notion of a gay church is a contradiction in terms because the homosexual "fails to understand that the Spirit of God transforms all men into the moral image of Jesus Christ and not the church into the image of the gay world. . . . What the gay world needs is redemption, not reinforcement." Henry's suggestion would of course be considered an outrage in the gay church, especially because of the traditional evangelical connotations of the word "redemption."

Conservative Christian spokesmen assert that the position in which the gay church finds itself trapped erroneously assumes that valid, relevant Christian ethics derive from and rely on human authority. Bockmühl writes:

> The unwarranted presupposition that homosexuality is heredi-
> tary . . . leads to the unsound practice of using statements made
> by "constitutional" homosexuals as the basis for ethical norms.
> This overlooks a fundamental fact: Christian ethics is prescrip-
> tive, not descriptive, or, to put it another way, Christian ethical
> standards are the product not of statistical research but of
> revelation (p. 17).

The latter statement is in contradistinction to an editorial appearing in a recent issue of *Commonweal,* which suggested that the church should "require its theologians to cooperate with sex researchers, other medical and social scientists, and hetero- and homosexual Christians in a new effort to reformulate guidelines for Christian sexual behavior" (April 6, 1973).

Advocates of "situation ethics" stress that homosexuality is not in itself sinful. "It all depends," Norman Pittenger says in *Christian Century* (December 15, 1971, p. 1469). In the same article he admits that he does not consider sin "to be a violation . . . of a moral law imposed from on high." Conservatives, on the other hand, believe that the law of God as revealed in Scripture is perfect because it reflects the nature of God. The moral character of God is unchangeable, and any "adjustment" of his proscriptive directives with regard to homosexual behavior is unacceptable. Because of their view of the absolute morality of God's Word, biblically orthodox churchmen reject the suggestion of leading gay spokesmen and liberal non-gay theologians that a primary task of today's "relevant" church is "rehabilitating Christian thinking about homosexuality."

In short, it appears that any reconciliation between straight and gay Christians will be limited to those groups at the more liberal end of the theological spectrum. Even so, it seems doubtful that rank-and-file straight church members will unquestioningly follow the thinking of some of their leaders. Since much of American Christendom is basically conservative, the gap between the gay church and the straight church will always be great.

Another major barrier between the gay church and the larger Christian church is the former's resistance to any discussion of change in a person's sexual orientation, or, put simply, of any form of "cure." Bockmühl observes:

> The remarkable and distressing thing is that not only have church spokesmen lost sight of the biblical condemnation of homosexual acts; they have also abandoned the biblical message of healing and restoration for those involved in homosexual sin on the same terms as for those involved in other types of sin. Thus "Christians" appear to be denying what many secular psychiatrists affirm, that homosexuality can be cured (p. 14).

As we have stated repeatedly, gay Christians view their sexual orientation as "God-given" and therefore any talk of a "cure" is ridiculed or ignored. Even fundamentalist gays who freely speak of Jesus "saving" them from sin become less than charitable, even hostile, toward those who suggest that Jesus can "deliver" them from homosexuality too. This is illustrated in an article published in the newsletter of MCC-Denver, in which Pastor Bob Darst responds to an article appearing in a "Jesus people" publication. The evangelistic appeal contains the following plea:

> Please listen though! We love you and Jesus really loves you! You can be cured! Many brothers and sisters have been set free already! There is hope! Jesus can change you completely. . . . We here at the Holy Ghost Repair Service want to see your broken life repaired by the power of God. . . (*The Catalyst*, Dec. 31, 1972-Jan. 14, 1973).

Darst calls those sentiments "highly offensive to every moral person, gay or straight, who is rational, aware, and not shackled by bigoted or Pharisaical attitudes."

> I agree [he continues] that Jesus does love us, but no true homosexual has to be "cured" in order to be welcomed into the Grace of God. The only criteria which God asks of us is that we believe and accept Him because we are justified by Faith alone. . . . A true homosexual can not be "cured" anymore than a black can become white or a one-legged man

suddenly grow a new limb. . . . Yes, Jesus can change your
life, but you do not have to change your life to come to Him.

The rejoinder of evangelical Christians would be that
Pastor Darst and his colleagues overlook the fact that
Jesus would have "accepted" homosexuals in the same
way that he accepted "publicans and sinners." It is true
that Jesus freely associated with those on the margins of
society, but none of these people came to Christ and
went away unchanged. The evangelicals are quick to
quote Jesus' injunction, "Go and sin no more."

Of course, gay Christians do not regard homosexual
behavior as "sin," so the dialogue reverts to an endless
cycle of arguments and counterarguments. It has been
our experience that gay Christians invariably respond
to accounts of cure — whether by psychiatric means or
evangelical conversion — with the explanation that the
person involved never really was a "true" homosexual.
They are forced to deny the veracity of apparently clear-
cut cases of cure, such as the following testimony from
David Wilkerson's magazine *The Cross and the Switch-
blade:*

> I was both a lesbian and a heroin addict. From the age of
> twelve, I used to have fantasies of being with another woman.
> . . . When I had sexual relations, I used to picture in my
> mind a woman making love to me. . . . I would be undressing
> different girls in my mind. . . . I was really into lesbianism.
> I was both a butch and a femme. I was planning to marry one
> of the girls I was living with, but was arrested for drugs and
> went to jail instead (June 1973).

The girl relates how she "cried out to God for help"
and became a "new creature" through Christ. "Not only
have I been delivered and set free from drugs, I've been
set free from lesbianism."

Psychiatrists point out that success in treating homosexuality by means of psychotherapy is largely dependent
on the motivation of the patient — he must strongly *want*
to change. Bockmühl echoes the same sentiment:

> Every healing in the Christian sense depends on the individual's
> answer to the question, *"Wilt* thou be made whole?" It is

necessary for him to admit the sin in his past life, make con-
fession, accept forgiveness, and begin to struggle *against* his
impulses and *for* the cause of Christ, under the guidance of
the Holy Spirit. . . (p. 17).

The apologists for gay liberation, on the other hand,
lump psychiatrists and religionists together as "the
raisonneurs of an oppressive society which systematically
deprives the homosexual minority of its civil rights
through harassment, ostracism, job discrimination, oppressive laws and imprisonment" (Driver, p. 104).

Most conservative Christians acknowledge a distinction
between a homosexual orientation (or propensity) and
homosexual practice. In his book, *The Returns of Love:
Letters of a Christian Homosexual,* Alex Davidson states
that ". . . while the practice is condemned [in the Bible],
the condition is neither condemned nor uncondemned;
it is not even mentioned" (p. 38). He asserts that the
Bible says nothing against the person who, for whatever
reason, is gay and who ". . . admits his inclinations but
keeps them strictly under control" (p. 41). Essentially
the same position is expressed in a letter to the editor of
Christianity Today written by a homosexual minister:

> I am a homosexual — but I am also a servant of the living
> Christ who experiences God's forgiveness and deliverance. By
> the grace of God this temptation does not express itself, and I
> am victorious through Christ (March 1, 1968, p. 23).

It is our opinion that the straight church is, in part at
least, responsible for the emergence of the gay church.
Gay churchmen are correct in the charge that conventional churches fail to minister to homosexuals. The
attitude of many Christians toward gay people is one of
repugnance and even contempt. It is perhaps revealing
that many gay pastors and parishioners come from fundamentalistic backgrounds and have attended Christian
colleges and churches where they found ignorance and
lack of information regarding their sexual problems.
Instead of Christian compassion, they experienced total
rejection. We agree with the Harvard psychiatrist

Armand M. Nicholi, who writes in the Foreword to *The Returns of Love* about the

> insensitive ear — not to mention the closed door — which the homosexual often encounters within the Christian community. Such rejection . . . intensifies the anguish, the pervasive loneliness and utter despondency that haunt the homosexual, and not infrequently lead to suicide. Christ, while taking strong action against sickness and sin, reached out to both the sick and the sinner with understanding and compassion. The church can ill afford to do less (p. 6).

Many of the gay ministers and lay people whom we met impressed us with their sincerity in attempting to deal with the spiritual problems of gay people. Often they have been able to minister to individuals who have had bad experiences with the institutional church and who perhaps had not darkened the door of a church in years.

Gay churchmen are fond of pointing out myths that straights hold about them, but gay Christians also have myths to unlearn about their straight counterparts. The chief example, we found, was the habit of gay Christians to lump together *all* conservative evangelicals as lacking in compassion, understanding, and Christian love. To listen to some gay church leaders, one would be led to believe that virtually all conservatives who disagree with them also believe that homosexuals are less than fully human, are not created in God's image, and that God could not possibly love a homosexual. This attitude is reflected in Troy Perry's frequent statement, "God Loves Me Too." Biblical, conservative Christians should be quick to counter that that fact was not in question.

Gay Christians need to recognize the honest sincerity of conservatives who admit that "the Christian Church has not shown any great ability to accept [homosexuals] . . . or to help them" (*Christianity Today,* January 19, 1968, p. 25). It is possible to demonstrate compassionate understanding of the homosexual's plight without having to discard sincere convictions about biblical norms — a position gay Christians evidently find untenable. The editorialist in *Christianity Today* goes on to describe what we hope will be the attitude of more and more Christians in straight churches:

> Christians have nothing to offer if they regard the homosexual as an untouchable, a sinner beyond the sphere of their concern. But they do him a disservice if they settle for less than the full biblical teaching about sex.

When a gay person is firmly committed to the conviction that his homosexuality is "God-given" and therefore not subject to change, his logical conclusion is that his life-style is just as desirable as the prevailing heterosexual way of life. Sometimes the suggestion is made that it might in fact be superior to heterosexuality (or that bisexuality represents the ideal, for it enables one to have the best of both worlds).

> Whether exclusive or near-exclusive homosexuality, even in the most sexually permissive society, can be as fulfilling to the individual as its reverse is open to doubt. Whether it can ever be, or should be, placed on a par with heterosexuality, without endangering the continued existence of the family, is more than questionable. Nevertheless, the stance of many spokesmen for the homophile movement is readily explicable. People trapped in a way of life require reinforcement of the value system that they are compelled to assume in order to gain self-acceptance (Sagarin, pp. 108-109).

The often cited "religious sensitivity" of homosexuals is part of the folklore surrounding gay people. Yet, in the gay church one is sometimes left with the impression that Christian gays actually believe that they experience something akin to an "added dimension" of spirituality because of their sexuality. Bockmühl quotes Karl Barth's observation that ". . . the first steps on the homosexual path can seem to 'shine with a special beauty and exotic spirituality, even with an aroma of sanctity'" (p. 17).

One final problem, then, facing the gay church is what to do about the body of evidence from the experience of humanity and from the biblical record that points to the conclusion that God ordained a heterosexual life-style for mankind culminating and being perpetuated in the man-woman relationship.

"We are *not* a gay church," says Pastor Larry Bernier of MCC-Boston. "We worship God like anybody else worships God, and the fact that we're gay has very little to do with it." The reader will have to determine the validity of that claim.

Selected Bibliography

Akers, Ronald L. *Deviant Behavior: A Social Learning Approach.* Belmont, California: Wadsworth Publishing Company, 1973.

Churchill, Wainwright. *Homosexual Behavior Among Males.* Englewood Cliffs, New Jersey: Prentice-Hall, Inc., 1967.

Davidson, Alex. *The Returns of Love: Letters of a Christian Homosexual.* London: Inter-Varsity Press, 1970.

Fisher, Peter. *The Gay Mystique.* New York: Stein and Day, 1972.

Gagnon, John H., and William Simon (eds.). *Sexual Deviance.* New York: Harper and Row, 1967.

Hoffman, Martin. *The Gay World: Male Homosexuality and the Social Creation of Evil.* New York: Basic Books, 1968.

Humphreys, Laud. *Out of the Closets: The Sociology of Homosexual Liberation.* Englewood Cliffs, New Jersey: Prentice-Hall, 1972.

Kinsey, Alfred C., Wardell B. Pomeroy, and Clyde C. Martin. *Sexual Behavior in the Human Male.* Philadelphia: W. B. Saunders, 1948.

Oberholtzer, W. Dwight (ed.). *Is Gay Good? Ethics, Theology, and Homosexuality.* Philadelphia: Westminster Press, 1971.

Perry, Troy D. *The Lord Is My Shepherd and He Knows I'm Gay.* Los Angeles: Nash Publishing, 1972.

Sagarin, Edward (ed.). *The Other Minorities.* Waltham, Massachusetts: Ginn and Company, 1971.

Weltge, Ralph W. (ed.). *The Same Sex: An Appraisal of Homosexuality.* Philadelphia: Pilgrim Press, 1969.

Wood, Robert W. *Christ and the Homosexual.* New York: Vantage Press, Inc., 1960.

Index